PRAISE FOR *TRAVEL LIGHT*

"*Travel Light* ultimately serves as a breath-of-fresh-air guide for how to be present in the modern day. Light's words and stories feel like a good friend that helps bring you back to your most important relationship when things get a little messy—the relationship with your Self."

Adriene Mishler
founder of Yoga with Adriene and Find What Feels Good

"*Travel Light* encourages readers to follow their curiosity, to live authentically to their inner guidance, and to always make decisions from the heart. Then every day becomes a new opportunity to do something that changes the course of the rest of our lives."

Sharon Salzberg
author of *Lovingkindness* and *Real Happiness*

"Light has lived out of a backpack now for four years. This is not a stunt or a gimmick but the commitment of a serious man to living a life based on the truths of the Inner World and the infallible wisdom of the heart. *Travel Light* is the best possible portal—and Light Watkins, the most generous and soulful guide—to this experience and this discipline. Can I give *Travel Light* six stars?"

Steven Pressfield
author of *The War of Art*

"This book is full of simply told, relatable stories that will leave you inspired to start traveling light on your very next trip."

Leon Logothetis
author and creator of *The Kindness Diaries*

"Light is a true master at taking complex practices like meditation and minimalism, and not only simplifying them but inspiring you to try them as well. *Travel Light* is a must-have for every spiritual practitioner."

Chip Conley
bestselling author and founder of the
Modern Elder Academy

"*Travel Light* is a concentrated distillate on all things simple whenever your life feels bloated, creaky, and full. Take two pages and call me in the morning."

Neil Pasricha
bestselling author of *The Book of Awesome*

"Light's unique approach to minimalism is so refreshing. This is just the book for showing you how to move through life in a way that truly serves what's in your heart."

Kute Blackson
bestselling author of *The Magic of Surrender*

"After reading and inhaling the message of *Travel Light*, for the first time in my life I traveled to Europe with a carry-on, inspired by Light's philosophy and way of living. I found the joy of letting go of excess baggage inwardly and outwardly. Read this book, and then give it away to a friend, and carry it in your heart. It will free your mind and spirit!"

Agapi Stassinopoulos
bestselling author of *Speaking with Spirit*

"Light is such a great storyteller. You can crack *Travel Light* open to any page, and before you know it, you will be inspired to give this unique style of minimalism a try."

Lewis Howes
author and founder of *The School of Greatness*

"*Travel Light* reminds us that our most important possession is our inner guidance. And that when we make room to follow that voice within us, we become aligned with the true abundance of life."

Ava DuVernay
award-winning filmmaker

"Light is speaking my language in his beautiful new book. Spiritual minimalism is a much-needed antidote to our seemingly endless scramble to get somewhere, to be someone, and to make things happen. Our harried, busy, distracted lives are not only bad for the planet but also bad for us. Thanks, Light, for directing us on a different path."

Pam Grout
#1 *New York Times* bestselling author of
E-Squared and nineteen other books

"It's so easy to get hung up on mental clutter. In *Travel Light*, my friend Light Watkins not only shows you how to declutter your mind but also provides you with step-by-step instructions for connecting with your inner guidance to live a more fulfilled life."

Mark Hyman, MD
bestselling author of *Young Forever*

Travel Light

Also by Light Watkins

Knowing Where to Look

Bliss More

The Inner Gym

Travel Light

Spiritual Minimalism to Live a More Fulfilled Life

LIGHT WATKINS

sounds true
BOULDER, COLORADO

Sounds True
Boulder, CO 80306

Published 2023

Cover design by Linsey Dodaro
Jacket and book design by Charli Barnes
Art by Simona von Woikowsky © 2023 Light Watkins

Printed in Canada

BK06622

Cataloging-in-Publication data for this book
is available from the Library of Congress.
ISBN: 978-1-64963-056-8
Ebook ISBN: 978-1-64963-057-5

10 9 8 7 6 5 4 3 2 1

To my rays of light:
Dustin, Levi, Kelie, Rian,
Demi, Drew, and Nile

Contents

Introduction

> "No matter what you have in your bag, if you
> cannot adapt to change, then you will always
> be carrying that around with you."
>
> **—The Spiritual Minimalist**

TURNING ON THE LIGHT

I flipped the switch, but there was no light. It was January 2022, and I had just returned to my Mexico City Airbnb from a week-long meditation retreat that I'd been facilitating. I set my daypack down on the couch and began investigating. None of the other light switches were working. Evidently, the electricity was out, which meant that I would not have the ability to wash clothes, charge my phone or tablet, use Wi-Fi, turn on the floor heaters, or do much of anything other than sit in darkness until it was time to go to sleep.

I notified the apartment manager right away. She had no idea why the power wasn't working in my unit even though it was on throughout the rest of the building, and she verified that the electricity bill was current. Regardless, she promised to have the power restored right away. Later that night, I received a message informing me that she hadn't had any luck with the electric company and that she would try again tomorrow.

This was obviously not a life or death situation. In fact, some would refer to it as a "first-world problem," barely worth mentioning. However, if you're not prepared for a relatively small change of expectation like this, losing access to power for even a couple of hours can be detrimental to your entire day, especially if you've just returned from a trip with clothes to wash, or food to cook, or a meeting to prepare for, with devices that need recharging. But luckily, I had been preparing for this kind of situation ever since I began intentionally practicing minimalism on May 31, 2018, the day I started traveling *light*.

My leap of faith into minimalism officially began when I turned in my thirty-day notice to the landlord of my two-bedroom Venice Beach apartment after a whole year of thinking about doing just this. I then contacted my car dealer and made an appointment to return my leased car at the end of the month. Next, I posted a series of classified ads online, listing all of my furniture, my Vespa scooter, and everything else of value that I no longer needed.

After doing some research, I found out that twenty-two inches was the largest carry-on bag allowed in the overhead compartment on most airlines. So I went to the luggage store to inspect the latest carry-on bags. I brought a bunch of clothes, accessories, and toiletries to see how much would comfortably fit into whichever carry-on bag I was considering. I left the store a couple of hours later with a brand new, high-end, twenty-two-inch carry-on bag.

This carry-on would effectively be my new apartment because, over the following month, I methodically cleared my apartment of everything that wouldn't fit into my bag. There would be no storage room, either, as I was allergic to paying a few thousand dollars a year to store items that I would likely forget about within a few months. On May 31, I rolled my new "carry-on" apartment out of my old, empty apartment and set out on my nomadic adventure.

A couple of years and dozens of destinations later, I scaled down to an even smaller backpack. And a year after that, I traded my backpack for a smaller daypack. In this process of elimination, I discovered one of the principles of what I began referring to as "Spiritual Minimalism": the fewer options you have, the more freedom you have to make decisions, and the more present you become.

I currently have around thirty items in my daypack, which include:

1 button-down shirt	1 pair of sandals
1 pair of pants	Toiletries
2 pairs of shorts	Refillable water bottle
3 pairs of underwear	Meditation shawl
3 T-shirts	Meditation teaching kit
1 jacket	Tripod
1 hoodie	Podcast microphone
1 sweatshirt	Rechargeable battery
1 belt	Tablet
1 pair of casual sneakers	Journal
1 pair of shoes	Mala beads

With these items, I've managed to travel the world two or three times over, giving talks; speaking on panels; leading workshops and retreats; working out each day; swimming, running, and hiking; going on dates; attending church, funerals, weddings, graduations, dinners, premieres, beach trips, celebratory gatherings, hot air balloon rides—you name it.

Back to Mexico City: it ended up taking my apartment manager two days to restore power. But it was only a mild inconvenience, because by that point—four years since becoming home-free—I had grown accustomed to operating with maximum efficiency and had trained myself to perform my most important daily tasks *without* relying upon electricity or even light.

For instance, many people, after returning from a week-long trip, arrive back home with a couple of suitcases full of dirty clothes that they need to wash immediately in order to have something to wear the next day. They also need a haircut. Maybe a shower. And they need to do some work on their phone or laptop, which likely needs to be recharged.

When I arrived back at my Airbnb, my daypack was already full of fresh, clean clothes that I had hand-washed on each night of my retreat. I was thoroughly practiced in shaving my head, even in the dark, without the need for a mirror, just in case I encountered this type of situation. I had already practiced doing everything I needed to do work-wise from my phone, including editing my website, composing complex newsletters, and writing this book. And I carried a portable charger with me everywhere I went in the event that there was no available power outlet to recharge.

What would have been considered major inconveniences were fairly minor thanks to my years of intentional preparation and practice. In fact, I kind of enjoyed having nothing to do in the evenings while navigating my apartment by candlelight. Of course, I didn't admit that to the apartment manager because I wanted her to get the power restored as quickly as possible.

But I was okay with the situation, and because I had cultivated fulfillment inside, I was able to focus on the opportunities as opposed to the few minor inconveniences, making the score for that day Unexpected Change = 0, Spiritual Minimalism = 1.

THE INSIDE-OUT APPROACH

When considering a minimalist lifestyle, you may be excited to quickly get rid of half or three-quarters of your belongings, or to follow my example and purge *any* item that doesn't fit into your carry-on bag or daypack. After all, that's what minimalism is all about, right? Minimizing your life? Creating space?

If that's primarily how you're interested in approaching minimalism, I've got some good news for you: there are dozens of books that offer very methodical approaches to cleaning out your closets, hosting yard sales, and acquiring new items with more intention—but *Travel Light* is not one of them.

I will not be going room by room with expert tips for getting rid of your old books, or the shoes you no longer wear, or that blender you haven't used for three years. Instead, *Travel Light* will provide you with instructions for exploring a less obvious but more individualized approach to minimalism, which I call "Spiritual Minimalism."

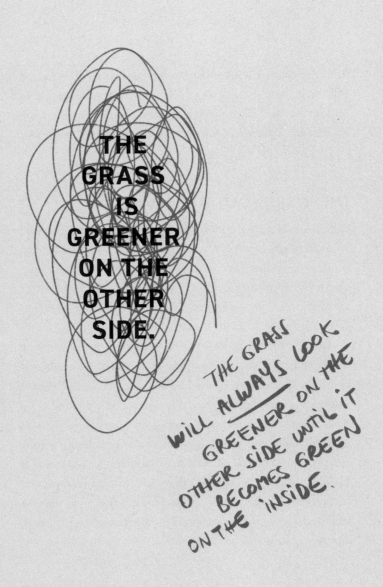

THE
GRASS
IS
GREENER
ON THE
OTHER
SIDE.

THE GRASS WILL ALWAYS LOOK GREENER ON THE OTHER SIDE UNTIL IT BECOMES GREEN ON THE INSIDE.

Spiritual Minimalism is more of an inside-out approach than the conventional outside-in approach to making space. In other words, this is not the get-rid-of-my-stuff-to-be-happy approach to minimalism. Rather, this is the get-happy-inside-*first*-and-see-what-happens-after-that approach to minimalism.

To illustrate the difference between the two approaches, let's run a quick thought experiment: Suppose you only had two weeks to become a minimalist—how would you proceed? We can imagine that most people would start by frantically going through their closets and getting rid of the items that they no longer use or need. Nothing wrong with that, but the Spiritual Minimalist would take a different approach. The Spiritual Minimalist would spend those first few days getting quiet enough to hear or feel in which direction their inner guidance was pointing them as the best path forward. Maybe it would be to clean out the garage. Or it could be to pull the plug on a friendship that is no longer serving them. Or to finally commit to an exercise routine.

Whatever the Spiritual Minimalist hears internally as a first step, no matter how illogical it may sound to the conventional minimalist, they trust it enough to start moving in that direction. A Spiritual Minimalist makes the majority of their decisions from their own *inner* guidance. And the best way to make sure your inner guidance is providing you with the highest quality information is to turn up the volume on what I call your "heart voice" through practices like daily meditation.

Conversely, the *less* connected you are to your heart voice, the more likely you are to make the majority of your decisions based on logic and external factors. This approach is not wrong. It's just not as efficient, because your heart voice is like your very own internal GPS. And not listening to it is a lot like ignoring the GPS in your car while it's attempting to guide you to your destination. You can still find your way using external signs, but it's going to take you longer, and you'll potentially make more mistakes along the way.

Your internal GPS is not just for arriving at destinations. It's also useful for knowing what to hold onto in your life and what to let go of. And the less access you have to your internal GPS, the more likely you are to ignore your gut instincts and the red flags warning you that certain relationships, material possessions, or experiences may no longer be relevant for where you're going.

So, while your closet may be tidy, if you're clinging tightly to a toxic relationship because you're afraid of being on your own for a while, then you may look like a minimalist in appearances, but you won't feel like one emotionally or spiritually. And which is more important? Looking like a minimalist, or actually embodying the principles of minimalism?

A Spiritual Minimalist becomes a specialist in listening to their heart voice, not because they were born with some unique ability to hear it, but because they invested sufficient time and effort to cultivate a reliable connection to it. And as a result, the Spiritual Minimalist will have an easier time letting go of whatever's been holding them back personally, professionally, or even spiritually, in order to create space for new experiences that are more aligned with their values and purpose.

This means that as a Spiritual Minimalist, you don't need to get rid of anything. What matters more than clearing out your closets is how much trust you have in your inner guidance and that you treat life as if there are no throwaway moments, give what you want to receive, follow your curiosity, are able to find comfort in discomfort, and embrace the freedom of choicelessness whenever possible.

All of those are foundational principles of Spiritual Minimalism, and each will be explained in detail throughout this book, using stories, anecdotes, and vignettes—many from my personal experiences as a practicing Spiritual Minimalist— along with real-world exercises that you can use to embody the Spiritual Minimalism mindset, without having to give anything away.

THE SEVEN PRINCIPLES
OF SPIRITUAL MINIMALISM

1. **Prioritize and cultivate inner happiness.**
   True inner happiness does not come from achieving
   future goals, acquiring experiences, or even from
   getting rid of your belongings. According to
   happiness research, once your basic needs are met,
   your baseline level of happiness will not significantly
   increase by acquiring more experiences, presumably
   including the experience of minimalism. But it
   is possible to increase your inner happiness by
   practicing certain *inner* exercises—such as stillness,
   gratitude, and giving. I'll show you how to do
   the most important one, which is stillness, in an
   enjoyable way. Once you begin hearing your heart
   voice through daily meditation, any confusion
   about your path will begin to clear up, and it will
   feel much easier to follow. This will lead to a greater
   sense of fulfillment because you will be able to more
   easily identify what you're here to do—and more
   importantly, what's *not* for you.

2. **Make your most important decisions from your
   heart, not your head.** To follow this principle, you
   must practice getting "out of your mind" (literally)

and into your heart as much as possible. After you begin tuning into the language of your heart, you'll start noticing the difference in your heart guidance and the other internal voices that may be instructing you to play small and fit in. You will also be shown how to split-test those internal voices in order to identify which one is the real voice of your heart and which ones are the impostors. And you will be encouraged to scale back on consciousness-dimming substances (for a period of time) and replace them with activities that provide you with a natural high, which will help to further clarify your true heart voice.

3. **Live as though there are no throwaway moments.** What if the best parts of your life—the ones you will ultimately tell stories about to your grandchildren— are happening right now, in small, seemingly insignificant moments? As you begin to show up more fully for the in-between moments, your life will naturally feel more fulfilled and aligned. You will also begin to treat every day like it's your birthday and every moment as though it holds a surprise gift for you. You will start to love and appreciate both giving and receiving small gestures of kindness, which will lead to more fulfillment with small things and an overall need for less.

4. **Give what you want to receive.** It doesn't matter how much or how little you have. If you want a friend, you must first be friendly. If you want love, you must be loving. If you desire abundance, you must live abundantly. If you're broke, you should be spending more money instead of trying to hoard it. And if you want generosity, you must lead with generosity. As you learn to embody this principle, you will naturally place less value on the things in your life and more on where you are investing your attention and presence.

5. **Your curiosity is the gateway to your path.** Your path is connected to that which you are already naturally curious about. And to live in alignment with your path, all you have to do is start following your curiosity without judgment. I will show you how to identify and explore your curiosity and how following it will make your day-to-day experiences as a Spiritual Minimalist more adventurous and fulfilling. And as your path requires you to take leaps of faith, you will begin to notice how your security is not sourced from external circumstances but from the internal trust that as long as you stay loyal to your curiosity, the dots will connect and you will always find yourself in the right place and at the right time (for you).

6. **Get comfortable with discomfort.** In order to fulfill your true potential, you will have to constantly confront and grapple with discomfort—whether it be psychological, emotional, or physical. The more comfortable you can make yourself with discomfort now, the more resilient you will be when you experience the turbulence of your next spiritual growth spurt—and the less tempted you will be to try and control life, run from it, or allow yourself to be defeated by it. Instead, you will learn how to transcend discomfort by experimenting with various Spiritual Minimalism practices that are designed to help you actively choose growth and find comfort in the most uncomfortable situations.

7. **Embrace the freedom of choicelessness.** You will challenge the conventional notion that having more options is better, and instead you will embrace the freedom of having only one option in most situations. Besides, the real freedom you are after is not about how many more choices you have. It's about cultivating the inner awareness to know at any moment which option is most aligned with your values. This will be a side effect of the iron-clad trust you develop in your heart voice.

CHOOSE YOUR OWN ADVENTURE

In this book, you will find a chapter dedicated to each of the seven principles of Spiritual Minimalism. At the start of each chapter, I will illustrate that particular principle of Spiritual Minimalism with a story or two, followed by an action step and other examples of that principle in action, using vignettes, anecdotes, photos from my personal journey, and illustrations. Concluding each chapter will be a peek into my daypack to see which items have become staples along my own Spiritual Minimalism adventure. As you'll notice, all of my items serve multiple purposes, which is a trademark of a Spiritual Minimalist—always searching for creative ways to do more with less.

The idea of showing you what's in my daypack is not to inspire you to emulate me, or to go out and buy anything, or to give up your worldly possessions. The idea is to show you how I think about what I carry as a Spiritual Minimalist. And then, maybe, you can adapt that thinking to your unique version of Spiritual Minimalism, as no two Spiritual Minimalists operate in the same way.

As with my previous book, *Knowing Where to Look*, *Travel Light* is presented in a choose-your-own-adventure style, which means you are invited to flip it open at random and read whatever story or anecdote catches your eye. As an aspiring Spiritual Minimalist, imagine that your inner guidance is dictating which page you land on. In that way, *Travel Light* is designed to simulate how a Spiritual Minimalist actually moves through the world, allowing your curiosity to guide you from place to place, from interest to interest, from conversation to conversation. So enjoy the open structure of this book, and only follow the suggestions that feel aligned with your values. Of course, you can read it cover-to-cover if that's what your inner guidance is directing you to do.

I've also added references to pages with related content in case you prefer to dive deeper into a particular aspect of Spiritual Minimalism. And if not, feel free to continue flipping around. Even if you have little or no interest in practicing minimalism, I've written this book to give aspiring minimalists and non-minimalists alike a fresh take on the subject that is sure to provide both groups with novel ways of living a more fulfilled life.

Also, remember that the suggestions in this book are not meant to lead to an overnight transformation, which is not sustainable anyway. The process of exploring Spiritual Minimalism is more about the journey than the destination. So relinquish your attachment to the timing and outcome and try as much as you can to enjoy the process. After all, that's what a Spiritual Minimalist is at the end of the day: someone who relishes the process of living life while allowing the outcome to be whatever it is—and knowing that on a divine level, life is always happening *for* them and not merely to them.

Additionally, *Travel Light* will help you tap into who you are beyond your titles, your accomplishments, your fears, your personality, and your stuff. It will help you create a safe internal space for allowing yourself to be guided along *your* unique path toward your highest potential. And as you explore these principles and put them into daily practice, you will have a more fulfilling (and perhaps minimal) life—one that you created from the inside out, which will make it unique to you.

In other words, you'll learn to give less importance to methodically getting rid of possessions, cleaning out your closet, or living life differently, and more importance to connecting with your *true* self (the part of you that is not concerned about outside opinions) and allowing that connection to determine what happens next. Maybe it'll be cleaning out your closet or downsizing to a capsule wardrobe, or it could be trading your home for an RV and traveling across the country.

It's not possible to predict how it will play out for you. All I know is that whatever happens as a result of you experiencing this book and implementing the principles of Spiritual Minimalism that feel aligned with your values, it's going to lead to a life-changing adventure!

PRINCIPLE 1:

Prioritize and Cultivate Inner Happiness

"If you're not spiritually secure, it does not matter how financially secure you are. It will always feel like you don't have enough."

—The Spiritual Minimalist

THE LONELY WAVE

A lonely wave had grown exhausted from having to aggressively maintain its wave-survival behaviors. After all, an isolated wave must work hard to coexist among bigger, richer waves, and spends most of its time protecting itself from danger and speculating about what all of the other, more powerful waves are up to.

Hearing about the lonely wave's woes, a fearless wave approached and offered the lonely wave some sage advice: "You should try de-exciting."

"Why would I want to do that?" asked the lonely wave. "Shouldn't I be figuring out how to get bigger so I can be as intimidating and powerful as those bigger waves?"

"Perhaps. But try de-exciting first," answered the fearless wave with a knowing smile.

The lonely wave decided to heed the wise wave's advice and began trying to de-excite. It wasn't used to intentionally getting smaller. But all it had to do was try less, and it naturally began to shrink. Gradually, it lost its boundaries. And without realizing it, the lonely wave became one with the ocean.

After a while, it reemerged with glee. "Wow, that was very interesting," it reported back to the fearless wave. "I've never felt so connected before. It was like I was a part of something bigger than myself."

With enthusiasm, the lonely wave repeated this practice of de-exciting over and over, day after day. And sure enough, the lonely wave began developing an inner trust and security that it had never before experienced, simply by doing less. And as a consequence, it felt less lonely.

When the lonely wave wasn't intentionally de-exciting, it became more relaxed in those moments when things didn't go its way. It ceased to make fear-based choices, and it felt a strange yet familiar connection to all of the other waves—even the bigger waves—making them seem less intimidating and scary.

The more it practiced de-exciting, the more it began operating from its true nature—its oceanic nature—and the more it realized that it had never been just a lonely wave amongst all of those bigger, more powerful waves. Instead, it was really the mighty ocean, expressing itself as an individual wave.

YOU ARE SPIRIT

From the Spiritual Minimalist perspective, you are Spirit (the ocean) being expressed as a human (a wave). And when you make the time and effort to lose awareness of your individuality through the process of de-exciting on a regular basis (via meditation), you will gain awareness of your true spiritual nature. This connection with Spirit will make it easier for you to embody the other six principles of Spiritual Minimalism:

- Make important decisions from your heart
- Treat life as if there are no throwaway moments
- Be willing to give what you want to receive
- Follow your curiosity
- Get comfortable with discomfort
- Embrace the freedom of choicelessness

As a result, you will begin to live a more fulfilled life, because those leaps of faith that once seemed too scary to seriously consider will appear less scary and more doable. The decisions that were once shrouded in uncertainty will be easier to make (such as, "Should I clear out the old to make room for something that feels more aligned?"). By plugging into your inherent strength of Spirit, you will become more and more fearless in *all* that you do and in all that you are. And you will realize that who you are at your core is already perfect, whole, and complete (like the ocean).

You won't need validation by acquiring more than you already have. You won't need to keep up with the Joneses anymore. You won't succumb to retail therapy as easily. In fact, you may be inspired to live with less. Much less. And it's not that you have to live with less in order to be free. It's that by embodying these principles, you will *feel* free. As a result, you will naturally want to lighten your load and live differently from the version of you who felt empty or who needed to acquire more stuff and experiences to fill the void.

With that inside-out perspective shift, you will naturally be more attracted to simplicity in all areas of life, and you may find yourself becoming more mobile, more minimal, and more adaptable to change. And because you will be less worried about losing your stuff, you'll become more willing to lead, to speak your truth, and to show up authentically in all areas of life.

ACTION: MAKING CONTACT

In order to allow yourself to be led by your spirit, you have to first make regular contact with your spirit and cultivate a relationship with your inner guidance—or what the ancient spiritual traditions refer to as the "still small voice." This is not an easy feat, because there are so many competing voices inside of us, especially when we sit to meditate. And that's one of the reasons why so many people prefer not to sit with their eyes closed for any significant length of time. All of those competing voices can make the experience feel quite unbearable.

It's a bit like an athlete in a sports arena trying to focus on playing their sport, but finding themselves getting distracted by everyone in the stands yelling and shouting at them about which moves to make. In this analogy, the still small voice would be the equivalent of those fans sitting all the way up in the nosebleed section, which would be barely audible to the athlete on the floor. Meanwhile, the fear-based voices and the voices of social conditioning all have floor seats, only because we've made a habit of listening to them and heeding their warnings throughout our life. That's why those fear-based voices often seem the loudest when we first start meditating. Those are also the voices that make us conclude that we have a "monkey mind" and that we are incapable of meditating.

But the entire point of daily meditation is to get the still small voice (also known as the "heart voice") to switch places with the fear-based voices. In other words, you can't get rid of any of the voices, nor can you stop your thoughts by thinking about not thinking, or by witnessing your thoughts like clouds in the sky, or by focusing on just the positive thoughts. But what you can do, with time and practice, is allow the meditation to turn up the volume on the still small voice, which is the thoughts that encourage you to be your most authentic self, to do the right thing, to lead with love, and to show up fully to the moment.

As you begin to hear your still small voice more clearly, you will have a much easier time following it. And it will be easier to treat the other voices that are telling you what *not* to do (and to play small, and to pretend like you're feeling differently from how you're truly feeling, and to disassociate from your emotions, and to contract in one way or another) like the background noise that they deserve to be—not the voices running the show. It's not important at this point to know which voices are which. What's important is that you focus on building a *daily* meditation practice, and the switch will gradually occur with time and experience. You will learn to verify that the switch has indeed happened by the quality of your day-to-day choices.

HOW TO MEDITATE

I've been practicing meditation for twenty minutes, twice a day, like clockwork for over twenty years. What made the biggest difference for me was having a teacher who taught me a very minimal approach to meditation—one that allowed me to sit comfortably and accept my mind as it is. Out of all of the meditation techniques I've tried over the years, the approach I learned from my teacher was by far the least complicated and, ironically, the most impactful.

**The ten steps for meditating
like a Spiritual Minimalist**

1. As early in the day as possible, sit with comfortable back support (you don't need to be on the floor).
2. Set a gentle alarm (such as a chime) for fifteen to twenty minutes.
3. Close your eyes.
4. Take three deep breaths, relaxing your body more with each exhale.
5. After the third deep breath, breathe naturally and maintain a friendly attitude toward your thoughts, no matter what they're about.
6. Use your natural breath as a soft, gentle anchor.

7. As your mind wanders from thought to thought, gently return to your breath (expect your mind to wander dozens of times in a single meditation).
8. Continue to breathe naturally throughout the process (there's no need to control or deepen your breathing).
9. When your alarm sounds, take three more deep breaths in and out of the nose or mouth.
10. After your third deep breath, slowly open your eyes.

Please Don't Overcomplicate It

Many new meditators love to complicate their practice by wondering if their palms should be facing up or down, or if their fingers should be together, or if they should have soft music playing in the background, or if they need an altar in front of them, or if they should be witnessing their thoughts like clouds, or visualizing a white light enveloping their body. The answer is no, no, no, no, no, and definitely not. Understand: you don't need to add *anything* to the ten steps. And whatever you're thinking of right now as an exception, you don't need to add that either.

You don't need to let go of anything, focus on anything, witness anything, notice anything, visualize anything, chant anything, resist anything, or intend for anything specific to happen. Don't focus on the still small voice, don't try to figure out what it's saying. Don't hold crystals that are supposed to help you connect to your inner guidance. Again, this is the Spiritual Minimalist approach to meditation. It's about stripping away any and all unnecessary elements. All you're essentially doing is practicing *being*, which is the opposite of doing. And with time and experience, you'll see how this approach does wonders for turning up the volume on your heart voice.

How long will it take? As long as it needs to take. For some people, it'll be weeks before they reconnect to their heart voice, and for others it may be months. The most important factor is consistency. **Do not skip your daily meditations.** How will you know it's working? You'll know by the quality of your decisions. You will start choosing to follow your heart, unprompted, more often than not, as opposed to following your head, even when if feels scary to do so. But we'll talk more about that when we discuss the next principle, which is all about following your heart. For now, you need to be able to hear what your heart is saying. Otherwise, you can't properly follow it. And that's what your daily meditation practice is going to help you do better than journaling, therapy, exercising, or anything else you may be doing to help you listen to and follow your heart.

THE NATURE OF YOUR MIND

In 2018, I published a book on meditation called *Bliss More*. I wrote it for people who believe in the power of meditation but who aren't sure how to meditate in a way that feels enjoyable. In the book, I teach what I call the E.A.S.Y. approach to meditation. E.A.S.Y. is an acronym for Embrace, Accept, Surrender, and Yield. Those are suggestions for how to treat your thoughts in meditation—for optimal enjoyment. If the number-one complaint of meditators is having a "busy mind," then the best way to neutralize it is by refusing to treat your mind as the enemy of meditation. As you cultivate a friendlier relationship with your thinking mind during meditation, you will discover that your noisiest thoughts gradually become less intrusive.

That means you'll hopefully stop referring to your beautiful mind as a "monkey mind," which is how many novice meditators describe their mind in meditation. It's popular to liken the mind to a drunk monkey with epilepsy that's been stung by a bee, erratically swinging from branch to branch (or in the case of meditation, from thought to thought). And this association with a drunk monkey is what causes new meditators to thought-shame themselves throughout the practice—meaning, they blame their so-called monkey mind for sabotaging what would've otherwise been a blissful experience.

But the reality is that your mind is not broken, it's not corrupted, and it's certainly not a drunk monkey with epilepsy. The nature of your mind is to think thoughts—and a significant number of thoughts at that. According to research, the average person (meditator or not) experiences 60,000 to 90,000 thoughts each day, which equals somewhere in the range of three thoughts per second. So all of us, regardless of our gender, race, culture, or even previous experience with meditation, technically have a "busy" mind.

If that sounds like a lot of thoughts, consider this: you experienced dozens of thoughts in the twenty or so seconds it took you to casually read that previous eighty-nine-word paragraph. If you count at least one thought per word, then you had at least eighty-nine thoughts. But it probably didn't feel like anywhere close to that many thoughts, right? That's because you were focused on the task of reading, and most of those thoughts were related to that activity, which you've done countless times. So your mind filled in a lot of the information subconsciously with pattern recognition, the processing of familiar words, understanding sentence structure, and cross-comparisons, in addition to taking in the external variables such as the surrounding sights, noises, smells, tastes, and feelings. But that's how researchers came up with the 60,000+ thoughts-per-day figure.

Pero la realidad es que tu mente no está rota, no está corrompida y ciertamente no es un mono borracho con epilepsia.

La naturaleza de tu mente es pensar pensamientos, y un número significativo de pensamientos. Según la investigación, la persona promedio (meditador o no) experimenta de 60 a 90 mil pensamientos por día, lo que equivale a un rango de tres pensamientos por segundo. Entonces, todos nosotros, independientemente de nuestro género, raza, cultura o incluso experiencia previa con la meditación, técnicamente tenemos una mente "ocupada."

The paragraph above is not a printing mistake. It's the same previous eighty-nine-word paragraph, but translated to Spanish. Did you try to read it? If so, did your mind feel busier even though the paragraph was expressing the same thoughts? If you don't understand Spanish, your mind will have a harder time recognizing patterns and will be flooded with thoughts about meaning, judgments about your lack of understanding, your slow progress, the negative ramifications of misunderstanding what you're reading, questions about why it's in Spanish, and so on. In other words, you will have the same number of thoughts, but the experience of navigating the foreign language will make your mind feel instantly busier, and your desire to give up will be exponentially greater.

This is essentially what happens in meditation. If you think of meditation as a foreign language, it's having the same effect. Because sitting with your eyes closed while doing nothing is so unfamiliar, it makes your thoughts feel more pronounced—because your mind feels lost. It's wandering. It's distracted. It's trying to understand what's being communicated. On top of that, you're being asked to intentionally *not* focus on any particular activity, sensation, or thought, and just be. But being can feel difficult (at first) because it's the cessation of doing, which is the state of action that we're used to, like our native tongue. With meditation, the mind doesn't have anything to compare being to or to label it with, other than "a waste of time" or "a boring activity" when contrasted with doing something "productive" or entertaining.

You may also feel like the volume of your mind in meditation is getting cranked up from a "normal thinking" level to a blaring "monkey mind" level, which blasts you with a series of what feels like loud, scattered, anxious, spastic, or even boring thoughts, many consisting of regrets from your past, conversations, song lyrics, random thought threads about completely unrelated experiences, sleepiness, goals and ambitions, and weird sensations. But here's the thing: it's all a part of becoming conversational in the language of meditation. As you practice being friendly with *all* of your thoughts as opposed to being combative or thought-shaming yourself, you will notice how these noisy thoughts gravitate to the back of your awareness, and the volume on them gets turned down, gradually leaving you with a more settled mind than the one you started the meditation with.

THE KRYPTONITE TO STRESS

In case you're thinking, *Light, I already meditate, and it hasn't made that big of a difference in my ability to hear my inner guidance*, what I've found is that the majority of meditators either have a loose relationship with consistency, or they are *doing* way too much when they meditate.

When I give meditation keynote speeches, I often start by polling my audiences to see what their frequency has been with meditation. I'll start by asking them to raise their hand if they meditate. And if there are one hundred people in the audience, usually around eighty hands will go in the air. Then I'll say, "Keep your hand up if you've meditated within the last twenty-four hours." And about half of those eighty hands will drop, leaving around forty in the air. Then I'll say, "Keep your hand up if you've meditated every day this week." And about half of those hands will drop, leaving around twenty in the air. Then I'll say, "Keep your hand up if you meditated every day this past month," and almost all of the hands will drop except for maybe two or three. "Ahhh, so there are my *daily* meditators."

The point is, when you say you've been meditating, I'm not talking about every blue moon or even a few times a week. To get access to your heart voice, you *have* to become a *daily* meditator. No days off. No holidays, birthdays, or weekends away from meditation. That's because meditation is helping to get rid of the main thing that's blocking your access to your own heart voice: stress.

"Stress" is a catch-all term for anything that causes you to have a distressful reaction to an otherwise non-life-threatening demand, pressure, or change of expectation. In other words, whenever you become afraid, sad, angry, bored, or maniacal, your body thinks that you're being attacked, and it will automatically begin to initiate the fight-or-flight reaction, which helps to protect you from the potential threat.

In order to guard itself, your body saturates itself with a host of powerful (yet toxic) stress hormones that are responsible for stimulating additional strength and stamina for running and fighting. But if you experience these toxic biochemicals too often, it can lead to long-term feelings of anxiety, depression, and the inability to focus—which means your intuition gets muddled and you get cut off from your heart voice, which in turn leads to paralysis by analysis and perpetuates the anxiety.

In contrast, the restful hormones that get created and distributed through daily meditation are like kryptonite to stress. In other words, your body's fight-flight chemicals cannot survive or thrive in a nervous system that is saturated in the biochemicals that get released through a daily, seated, eyes-closed meditation practice. And as a consequence, it will become easier and easier for you to hear the voice of your heart over the noise created by decades of stress accumulation gone wild.

TROUBLESHOOTING YOUR MEDITATION PRACTICE

Is it possible to over-meditate?

Sure. But the far bigger issue is under-meditating. Ninety-nine percent of people have a harder time with consistency. Therefore, you don't have to worry about over-meditating. Unless you have a natural inclination toward monasticism, over-meditating is not going to be your problem. Just try to be consistent. Once daily for fifteen to twenty minutes is your aim.

How do I know if I'm meditating when I'm meditating?

The same way you know you're surfing (you're in the water), or dancing (you're on the dance floor). It's not about being an expert from day one or being able to quiet the mind on demand. Meditation is a process, and as long as you're sitting with the intent to meditate, then trust that you're meditating.

What percentage of time should my mind wander in meditation?

One hundred percent of the time. Trying to stop your mind from wandering in meditation is as futile as trying to stop your heart from beating by thinking, "Don't beat!" over and over. It's going to keep wandering, and therefore it's best to just shift your attitude about it from antagonistic to friendly. In other words, never chastise your mind for thinking. Instead, if you practice celebrating your wandering mind, it will become more settled more often.

How can I tell if the meditation is working?

Here are fifteen ways to know that your meditation is working beautifully, even when it does not feel like it.

1. You have more energy outside of meditation.
2. You're sleeping better at night.
3. You're less controlling in life.
4. You're able to see the silver lining in seemingly "bad" situations.
5. Your cup is more half-full than half-empty.
6. You're more fearless when it comes to following your heart.
7. You worry less.
8. You're more adaptable to change.
9. You take rejection a lot better.
10. You get sick less often.
11. You enjoy your own company a lot more.
12. You're more daring.
13. You prioritize self-care.
14. You're more decisive.
15. You're more present.

HOW IS MEDITATION
RELATED TO MINIMALISM?

Meditation will play a crucial role on your journey into Spiritual Minimalism by helping you access your heart voice. And it's your heart voice that tells you what's good for you and what to pass on. Imagine how much time you can save when you no longer have to deliberate over whether or not something is right for you.

With a higher level of discernment, you can be twice as effective as someone with double the amount of time, simply because you're receiving internal guidance in how to best optimize your time. This is what is meant by the spiritual axiom "do less to accomplish more." And that's why your ability to discern is crucial to your journey into Spiritual Minimalism. Your power of discernment will help you *feel* which items and experiences are relevant for you, which books to read, which places to visit, and who to invite along your journey.

When people don't have access to their power of discernment, they tend to prioritize the wrong things. And it's the accumulation of prioritizing the wrong things thousands upon thousands of times that will ultimately lead to experiences like poor health or being stuck in soul-sucking jobs or bad relationships. Those situations don't happen out of the blue or by accident. They happen from making poor decision after poor decision, where you lacked sufficient discernment, hundreds or thousands of times.

Of course, many people in these types of situations will deny that the outcome of their life is a direct result of their lack of discernment—but even their inability to see that connection also stems from a lack of discernment. So you can't escape it. And that's why meditation is not just important, but necessary, as few experiences can expand awareness more efficiently than sitting once or twice a day with your eyes closed for fifteen or twenty minutes and going within.

Once you commit to your daily practice, those connections that were previously invisible to you will begin to reveal themselves like those Magic Eye puzzles. And you won't have to read or watch videos about how useful meditation is because you'll finally be seeing for yourself by having the direct experience.

WHAT'S IN MY BAG: MY MEDITATION SHAWL

Meditation shawls are as old as the practice itself. Not only does your shawl make you come off as a serious meditator, but the Spiritual Minimalist knows how a trusty meditation shawl has utility beyond their daily practice.

The type of shawl I use is a pashmina, which is made of wool from the undercoat hair that goats shed naturally each spring.

The hair is traditionally combed off and collected by the Changpa people of the Himalayas. Ironically, the Changpa are a nomadic tribe.

I got my pashmina in Rishikesh, which is located in the Himalayan foothills of northern India. During the cooler winter months, I like to have my shawl nearby to stay nice and cozy in meditation. What I've found is that the less distracted you are by the temperature, the easier your mind and body will settle during meditation. In that sense, your shawl can significantly increase or decrease the quality of your practice.

Any shawl will do for the purposes of meditation, and pashmina shawls are extremely thin and easy to travel with, not to mention comfortable. While my shawl is primarily for meditation, it's not limited to that purpose.

Here are seven other ways I've used my trusty meditation shawl since becoming a daily meditator many moons ago, and a glimpse into what you're missing out on if you don't yet use a shawl for your daily practice.

As an extra cover

In case you're traveling and there's not enough warmth in the room, you can spread out your shawl in between your bed sheet and duvet for extra coziness.

As a nap blanket

After your daily meditation, if you need a little extra rest, just lie down (or slide down and rest your head back), and use your shawl as your blanket.

As an eye cover

If for whatever reason you'd like to turn the lights down in your room or on your plane, but you have no control over the light switch, you can gently wrap your shawl around your eyes, and it becomes the perfect eye mask for getting deeper rest.

As a mosquito net

We've all had that experience where it's the middle of the night, you're trying to sleep, but there's a mosquito buzzing around your ear. You can either start swiping into the darkness (hint: you're not going to get it), or you can put your trusty meditation shawl over your face. It's thick enough to protect you against mosquito bites but light enough to allow you to breathe.

As a fly protector

Are you meditating in a place with flies landing on you? If you haven't yet reached the state of enlightenment where bugs don't bother you, your meditation shawl can be a useful protector against that type of nuisance.

As a pillow

If you find yourself on a long flight and you are lucky enough to have a row all to yourself, you can ball your shawl up and use it as a pillow, or if you're sitting in a chair, it makes a perfect headrest.

As a makeshift robe

When you're up in the morning but you haven't gotten dressed yet, your shawl will keep you from offending anyone by walking around in your underwear (or with no underwear). Just wrap it around your waist or your chest like you would a bath towel.

If you aren't interested in a meditation shawl, the point of this "What's in My Bag" section is to think like a Spiritual Minimalist whenever you're purchasing or acquiring new items and consider all of the ways that your items can be used. That way, without even trying to minimize, you'll find yourself doing more with less if you ever feel inspired to travel lighter.

PRINCIPLE 2:

Make Decisions from the Heart

"*Not* following your heart is a form of self-betrayal—
which means whatever comes after that is on you."

—The Spiritual Minimalist

MY LEAP OF FAITH

Back in 2007, it was common to see hipsters congregating outside of my one-bedroom West Hollywood apartment to receive their personalized mantra from me. That was the year I started teaching Vedic meditation, and in the process, I became the neighborhood mantra dealer. My journey into teaching meditation required a series of bold leaps of faith, and I genuinely felt like I had found my calling.

I was making more money than ever before, doing something that I honestly would've done for free, while helping people in a way that felt authentic and aligned with my soul. By all

accounts, I was living my dream. And as if life couldn't get any better, later that year I met a beautiful young woman in a health-food store, and we entered into a loving relationship that culminated in us renting a charming little beach cottage in one of the most desirable neighborhoods in Venice Beach, California.

And then, only a few months after we moved in, for some inexplicable reason, my meditation teaching business began to dry up. I was gaining experience and becoming a better teacher, but people just stopped coming to learn. And here we had just moved into this much more expensive house, which put a lot of financial pressure on me to cover the bills.

Then, out of the blue, my girlfriend broke up with me and moved out of our house. I was stunned, sad, and overwhelmed because my rent essentially doubled overnight. Meanwhile, the bills were piling up—and I was now desperate to teach people how to meditate. And the few people who were coming to my free orientations could sense my desperation, so they weren't signing up for my paid training.

This was a very confusing time because, again, I felt deep down that I had found my path and was very much following my heart. And while things started off well, now I was questioning everything. Wasn't I meant to teach meditation? Was I supposed to move elsewhere? How would I pay my bills? Should I get a part-time job?

I'll never forget going online late one night and searching for part-time jobs around Los Angeles for $18 and $20 an hour. I would read the job descriptions: This job requires twenty hours a week of this or that kind of work, and you must be willing to commute to Brentwood, or Pasadena, or somewhere else far away from Venice Beach. And I remember sitting there trying to figure out creative ways to commute to a part-time job while still having the time to teach meditation whenever an opportunity arose. This wasn't easy because the meditation teaching opportunities could be so sporadic. But I kept searching for the right part-time job.

Then, something occurred to me (now I know it was my heart voice, but back then it just seemed like a flash of inspiration). I started thinking, *Man, I'm putting all this thought into figuring out how I can combine jobs and add value to someone else's business. But what if I invested that same creative energy into my calling? What if I spent those same twenty hours a week working intensely on becoming a better teacher, or on my marketing, or on some other aspect of my teaching business?*

And I started thinking about how I could add more value to the meditation space, which at the time was still in its infancy. My heart voice then said to get my point-and-shoot camera (this was before smartphones) and start shooting videos about different aspects of meditation—you know, answering frequently asked questions, helping to define terms like "consciousness" and "nirvana"—and start posting them on this website called YouTube, which had launched a few years earlier.

So over the next couple of days, I turned my living room into a video set. And every day I would shoot several three- to four-minute videos about various aspects of meditation and upload them to YouTube. The videos garnered modest views, and slowly my meditation teaching began picking back up— just enough to pay my major bills, but not much else.

Then, my heart planted the idea of organizing a meditation teaching trip in New York. Now this was scary because up until that point, I hadn't taught outside of Los Angeles. I had less than $1,000 to my name, and bills totaling around $3,000 to $4,000. So if I flew all the way to New York and it turned out to be crickets, I would be screwed because, on top of my flight, I would have to prepay for a teaching space as well as a place to stay, and incur other expenses with money I didn't have to lose.

Meanwhile, I remembered that some of my friends in New York had been begging me to come and teach them how to meditate—but I was suspicious that they wouldn't turn up if I actually came. And as I went back and forth between my fear voice telling me not to spend my remaining money on this trip where nobody was going to turn up, and my heart voice encouraging me to take the leap, I reluctantly decided that I had to follow my heart.

So I spent half of my last $1,000 on a plane ticket to New York and the rest on renting a place to teach. When I got to my "free" meditation orientation, sure enough, none of my friends who had been begging me to come to New York ended up showing up to the session. In fact, there were only about six people in the room out of the fifteen or so who had RSVP'd.

I tried not to show my disappointment and instead delivered my orientation as if I was speaking to a crowd of one hundred. Four of the six people ended up signing up for my paid training, which brought in about $6,000—more than enough to pay for the trip and cover my bills.

One of those students was a physical therapist who showed so much enthusiasm in the training that he invited me to return to New York to teach all of his clients from his physical therapy studio, which he offered to me for free, and assured me that he had dozens of affluent New Yorkers who would enroll in my training. I asked him how he had discovered my course. "I've been watching your YouTube videos."

This new collaboration revived my meditation teaching business. I went from not having enough money to pay my rent to teaching hundreds of students that year and becoming one of the top meditation teachers on both the West and East Coasts of America. My YouTube videos were continuing to gain traction, and more people were coming to learn—all thanks to following my heart voice.

I started facilitating workshops around the world. I organized and led sold-out retreats. I gave a TEDx talk that went viral. I started writing books. And I never had to look for a part-time job again. There were many takeaways from this experience, but the main takeaways are the following:

Number one, when your heart voice guides you in the direction of your purpose, the thing that helps you get started is not necessarily going to be the same thing that helps you sustain and grow your purpose. So you have to continually listen to and follow your heart while staying creative along your path. You will be scared for much of the time. But it's a good kind of fear that accompanies growth and expansion as opposed to a paralyzing fear.

Secondly, a leap of faith cannot be an isolated act. It must become a lifestyle. There may be a hundred leaps between where you are now and where you will be in five years, which means you will have to repeatedly trust that your heart voice will never lead you astray.

Next, if you feel like you're living your calling now yet you're not getting the resources or support that you need to make ends meet, you must begin to ask different questions. Instead of asking, "How am I going to pay my bills?" you have to also ask, "How can I be even more authentic in my approach?" And, "How can I help even more people in a more genuine way?"

And finally, if you're asking yourself those kinds of questions, which are the best questions to ask, then the answers that eventually come to you will reveal the steps for taking your calling to the next level. But you have to be quiet enough to hear the answers clearly (that's why meditation is key), and you have to be courageous enough to take whatever leap of faith your heart voice is prompting you to take next (which would be *your* version of flying to New York).

ACTION: SPLIT-TESTING YOUR HEART VOICE

We all have dozens of voices inside of our heads, each telling us what to do and how to do it. People assume that goes away when you start a daily meditation practice. But in truth, the myriad voices will remain in there, shouting and vying for your attention, each sounding more urgent and more important than the others.

However, one voice will become more distinct with consistent meditation: your still small voice of inner guidance, also known as your intuition, or heart voice. That's the voice that encourages you to take better care of yourself when you're busy, to do the right thing when it's inconvenient to do so, and to make the courageous choice even when the majority of people

are choosing the safer option. While meditation can't get rid of those other voices, it can turn up the volume on the heart voice to the point where it no longer feels too still or small to ignore—but loud enough to be heard clearly, convincingly, and to be acted upon.

Whenever I publish content related to following your heart, without fail I receive a barrage of comments and questions from readers claiming that they can't hear what their heart, or inner guidance, is saying. Not sure if you've ever felt like that, but the reason it could be difficult for you to hear your heart voice is because it's competing with so many other voices (of the ego, pain-body, fear, past trauma, and more). The trick is to do what successful entrepreneurs do with their internet marketing strategy and start intentionally split-testing those voices.

In other words, if there are multiple voices in there offering conflicting guidance, start following the voices that you think could be your heart voice and see if doing so leaves you feeling more inspired or less inspired. After conducting 500 or perhaps 1,000 such experiments, you'll eventually home in on which one is your true heart voice. That's the voice that nudges you in the direction of your potential, which is often away from your comfort zone and toward your growth zone—where you have no idea how things are going to turn out, but when you consider the best possible outcome, it makes you feel expansive. And that's one of the telltale signs that you're being guided by your heart voice.

Instructions for the split test:

Learning the language of your heart voice is a lot like learning a new language. As a child, it's obviously much easier to learn a new language just by being exposed to it. But as an adult, you must study that new language carefully and practice it intentionally, and you must be willing to make a lot of mistakes in an effort to become conversational in it.

Similarly, with your heart voice, you must study all of your internal voices and intentionally practice following the ones that you feel represent the true voice of your heart. You will of course make mistakes, and you may accidentally follow your ego voice or your fear-based voice at some points, but that's how you will learn to distinguish your heart voice from all of those other voices.

Here are some of the qualities you're looking for to identify your true heart voice:

Your heart voice won't tell you what not to do, only what to do. Example: your heart voice won't say, "Don't talk to that person." Instead, it may say, "Just be a good listener right now."

Your heart voice will prompt you to get out of your comfort zone. Example: you may feel tempted to sincerely compliment a stranger on their style. That's your heart voice prompting you, so go for it.

It will nudge you to be more courageous. Example: while in a group setting, you may be asked to stand up and share a personal experience that you've had that could help others, and your heart voice is the one saying, "Go ahead and just speak from your heart," while your fear voice may be urging you *not* to speak because what if you sound stupid?

It's the opposite of aversion. If you feel repelled by or afraid of a potentially embarrassing possibility, usually your heart voice is the one that's nudging you to face it. Left unchecked, the fear voice can run your life, because you've heeded its advice for so long. So if you're feeling the urge to run away from something that could be useful, helpful, or motivational (due to fear), try doing the opposite.

Other signs that you're hearing the voice of your heart: it's not letting you off the hook with what you decided to do to improve yourself or your corner of the world. It's encouraging you to take a leap of faith, to stay committed, and to keep investing in yourself and your purpose.

Signs that the voice you're hearing is *not* your heart voice: it's tempting you to quit instead of looking for other solutions, or to act in a way that would harm you or others, or to seek out a shortcut, or to search for an easier way so you don't have to get uncomfortable, or to play small, or to people please, or to apologize for being yourself, or to seek permission before following your heart, or to look for an external sign before acting on what you feel inside.

How to split-test your heart voice:
Start acting on what you suspect is your true heart voice.

If it says to go to the left while you're walking somewhere, then go left, even if going to the left takes you out of your way a bit.

If it says to grab a certain book from your bookshelf and flip through it, then follow it, even if you've got no interest in the subject of the book.

If it says to stop and smell a flower, then stop and smell the flower, even if you're running behind.

If it says to go up to an attractive person and ask for their number, do not hesitate to ask for their number. You can even blame it on this exercise if you're not feeling so confident.

Once you act on what you feel is the voice of your heart, notice how things turn out. If you find yourself in the right place at the right time, that's a good indication that you're following your heart voice. Here are a few other considerations to confirm that you're indeed listening to your heart voice:

The message was life-affirming. Successfully following it made you feel more empowered as a result.

It disrupted a part of your status quo that you've been complaining about. For example, if you've despised your job, the guidance of your heart voice prompted you to explore other possibilities.

It guided you to be the hero as opposed to the victim. Heroes act, victims react. If you were feeling called to be bold in action, then that was definitely your heart voice.

It placed you in a position to serve. Following it allowed you to help others in some meaningful and possibly unexpected way.

Try to act on your heart voice's guidance at least once a day, and keep on doing so until you become conversational in its language. The more familiar you become with your heart voice, the easier it will be to follow. And soon you'll start to see that your heart voice, as scary as it sometimes is to follow, always has your best interest at heart.

Eventually, you'll get the volume turned all the way up on your heart voice, to the point where it becomes a loud, annoying voice—like that of a roommate who is reminding you that you're two weeks late on paying your half of the electric bill, and who won't let you do anything else *until* you take care of the payment. Believe it or not, your heart voice can and will get that loud and annoying, and it won't let you do anything else until you follow it.

This is ideally where you want the volume of your heart voice to be. That way, you don't have to rely on motivation or inspiration to follow it—because chances are, you're really not going to feel like doing whatever it's urging you to do since it almost always takes you out of your comfort zone. But if it's loud enough, and annoying enough, you'll go with it. Granted, you may drag your feet, kicking and screaming, but you'll follow it, if only to shut it up.

And then you will become that person at parties and on road trips who has the most amazing stories to tell. And they'll all start with, "I was in this or that situation, and then *something* told me to . . . and I did it, and you won't believe what happened next . . ."

Warning: The thing that will make you postpone following your heart voice is a desire to know beforehand how everything will turn out. But the truth is, you can never know how it's going to turn out. You have to just leap into action and trust that it will turn out for the best. If you end up in what you consider to be an undesirable place, you can always leap again. And you can continue leaping as much as necessary, with the understanding that a legitimate message from your heart is going to take you out of your comfort zone and into your growth zone. As a Spiritual Minimalist, the more you act upon these inner cues, the less scary it will be to leave your zone of comfort.

MEDITATE ON IT

People have all kinds of advice about the best ways to achieve goals, but few understand how to determine which are the best goals to go after in the first place. That's because the answer can't be sourced externally. As a Spiritual Minimalist, you must go within. You must repeatedly establish yourself in being—ideally through meditation. You must become as familiar with your inner landscape as you are with your neighborhood. You must learn its contours and become attuned to its impulses, frequencies, and vibrations.

Furthermore, and most importantly, whenever you're at a crossroads, you should never try to *find* an answer. After a week or two of meditating each day with no particular outcome in mind, you will become settled enough to sense from deep within which path your heart voice is urging you to take. And just know that what feels aligned with your heart is also good for those who depend on you. So don't worry if others will be okay with your decision. They will be fine so long as you act in integrity with what you feel inside.

In time, the best answer, the right answer, the most evolutionary answer, will slowly come into focus. It's a process that can't be rushed, because it's occurring on divine timing—which means, if you've been investing time into your meditation and you still can't detect what your heart voice is saying, then the answer is not yet ripe enough for you to act on it. But once the answer crystallizes, you can assume it's ready for action.

Don't let fear make you second-guess yourself. Fear is a natural response to leaving your comfort zone. And a clear message from your heart will usually come with an element of fear. But there should be no more going back and forth.

No seeking a second opinion. No scheduling a reading with a psychic to verify if what you heard is correct. And you can forget about asking others what they think, because the answer is not going to make sense to anyone else—only to your heart.

So don't delay. You must act with urgency and complete confidence that you're on your path. After all, you followed the protocol to source the best answer, which was to establish yourself in being through meditation. Once the message is clear, it's time to act.

BECOMING PRO-AWARENESS

When you're new to following your heart, it can sometimes be difficult to distinguish between the noisy voices in your head and the wise voice of your heart. Even in the best conditions, when you're rested, healthy, and quiet, your heart voice can be difficult to decipher.

And one of the quickest ways to weaken your connection to your heart voice even further is by indulging in alcohol, because alcohol makes it even more difficult to hear what your heart voice is saying. If you sincerely want to turn up the volume on your heart voice, then I strongly recommend temporarily abstaining from alcohol.

If there was a polar opposite state to Spiritual Minimalism, it would be the state of inebriation. To be clear, practicing Spiritual Minimalism is not about being anti-alcohol. It's about being pro-awareness, and being willing to go to whatever lengths it takes to cultivate and protect your connection to your heart voice—including temporarily abstaining from alcohol if necessary.

Understand that if an inner voice tries to convince you that going a few months without alcohol is too long, or that a little wine here or a joint there isn't that big of a deal, or any other justification for rejecting the idea of sobriety, you now have hard proof that the loudest voice in your awareness is not the voice of your heart, because your heart would never try to justify dimming your connection to it with substances.

The question you must ask yourself is, if that other voice is defending your use of awareness-dimming substances so strongly, what else is it influencing you to do (or not do)? Because if it can easily sway you to reject the idea of going without alcohol, then it's possible that the same voice is blocking you from accessing your potential in other areas of your life.

Furthermore, we live in a culture that has normalized the regular consumption of alcohol—so much so that most adults in our society are functional alcoholics. Of course, very few functional alcoholics would consider themselves to be functional alcoholics. They only drink during the off hours, they would say in their own defense, or on the weekends. It's only a couple of drinks a week. They can stop anytime they want.

Yet alcohol is so prevalent in our society, most people would find it impossible to abstain. We drink when we celebrate a special occasion, and we drink when something bad happens. We drink to connect, and we drink because we're lonely. We drink when we're relaxed, and we drink because we're on edge. In other words, there's always a socially acceptable reason to drink.

So to focus on turning up the volume on your heart voice, I strongly recommend going at least three months without consuming alcohol. And if, after three months, you still decide to drink, at least you've given yourself a chance to become more heart-led. And in the process, you may realize that you don't need intoxicants in order to enjoy life, and that being grateful and present, and having clear access to your heart voice, gives you a deeper level of satisfaction than drinking.

Exercise

If the idea of establishing a stronger connection with your heart voice intrigues you, start abstaining from alcohol and recreational drugs for as long as you can, with the intention of working your way up to three months. Maybe you only get to a week before having a drink. That's fine. Just start over and see if you can make it to two weeks the next time. And keep starting over and extending the time until you make it to three months in a row. Take as long as you need. Over time, you will have enough exposure to your heart voice that you will be inspired to abstain for longer and longer. The entire experiment may take a year, but it is sure to be one of the most transformative years of your life.

The Spiritual Minimalist always seeks life-supporting, life-affirming actions and behaviors that deliver multiple positive benefits in various aspects of their life. Do less to accomplish more. If there are obvious negative side-effects or downsides to a behavior, then the Spiritual Minimalist defaults to looking for a more positive alternative that results in more awareness. Whenever there's a will to be more connected to their heart, the Spiritual Minimalist is committed to finding a way.

WHAT'S IN MY BAG: MY ACCESSORIES

While you are split-testing your heart voice, your heart may guide you to do all kinds of weird and curious things along your Spiritual Minimalist journey, such as jotting down a quote that inspires you, taking a photo of a tree that you feel a special connection with, wearing a certain accessory that invokes comments from passersby, taking the long route to your destination, or reading a book on a subject that is outside of your usual area of interest.

To prepare you for taking advantage of your many heart-led nudges and impulses, I recommend adding the following accessories to your Spiritual Minimalist bag: a good pen, a personal effect, a device for tracking your steps such as a smart watch or a smartphone, a pair of headphones, a tablet, and a backup charger. Each item has multiple purposes. Here are some details on how to get the most out of carrying less.

A good pen

Like everything we've been talking about, the medium is the message. As a Spiritual Minimalist, you want to leave places better than you found them, and sometimes that means leaving behind a sincere note of appreciation. You want your note to be written with a quality pen that has a nice, wide tip. If you watch some YouTube calligraphy videos, you can enhance your penmanship in an impressive way, which adds to the specialness of your thank-you note. You can also use your pen for journaling, signing receipts, writing down directions, or taking notes.

Mala beads

Since becoming a meditation teacher in 2007, I wear a string of 108 mala beads, which is one of the universal indicators that I do something related to spirituality. The type of beads and the way you wear them distinguishes which spiritual tradition you're a part of. My malas have become one of the accessories I wear to dress up my otherwise ordinary teaching outfit of T-shirt and chinos. If you throw on a mala, all of a sudden you have a look of spiritual distinction. My mala is extra-special to me because I hand-made it. But you don't have to get a string of mala beads to accessorize your capsule wardrobe. Perhaps there's another decorative accessory that resonates with you: a bracelet, a particular type of hat, a charm, a pin, a scarf. Whatever it is, it should be simple and light enough to carry, elegant yet not overbearing, and offer a unique way to dress up your capsule wardrobe (see my capsule wardrobe on page 178).

A smart watch

For years, I wore a Rolex. It was a gift from my brother that I cherished dearly. But the Rolex didn't have as much utility as I desired when I went nomadic. So I re-gifted it back to him before selling off all of my things, and I replaced it with a smart watch. One of the unexpected benefits of the smart watch was that I could use it to easily track my step count. And as the saying goes, what you measure, you can improve. So I began noticing how many steps I was taking on a daily basis—something I never paid much attention to before. Then I started seeing if I could increase my steps. Eventually, I aimed for 10,000 steps a day. As you'll read on page 128, the Spiritual Minimalist is a flaneur (someone who enjoys the art of walking aimlessly). And while it's not necessary to measure how many steps you take daily, or to use a smart watch to track your steps (most smartphones come with step-tracking apps), it's still fun to compare today's step count to yesterday's. Plus, the right smart watch can serve a dual purpose of dressing up your simple wardrobe.

A smartphone

Sure, you will need something to make calls on, but you will also need a device for listening to audiobooks and podcasts and for reading e-books—the primary way that Spiritual Minimalists consume books and other electronic media. Most people have smartphones, but you want a phone that also allows you to take photos and video. You want a reliable camera because the Spiritual Minimalist doubles as a documentarian, a journalist, and a content creator. To that end, you need a phone for documenting your journey, as the camera roll has become our modern-day diary. Plus, whenever someone hands you a business card or an important receipt, you're going to snap a photo of it as opposed to stuffing it into your wallet or purse.

Headphones

Get a pair of headphones that you can use for multiple reasons: to listen to audiobooks and podcasts, and obviously to talk privately on the phone. No one likes the annoying person who talks on speaker phone in public. That's not Spiritual Minimalist behavior, so never do that when others are around—at least not if you want to be welcomed back to that space. You can also use your headphones to avoid having conversations with other people, which is something I do all the time. I'll sometimes keep my earbuds in while walking around, and if I want to engage with someone I know, I'll take them out—but if I'm not in the mood to engage (for whatever reason) I'll motion that I am occupied and keep it moving. It's a simple way to protect your space while letting the other person save face.

A tablet

I got rid of my laptop several years ago, and now I just use an electronic tablet with a floating keyboard. In fact, I wrote both this book and my previous book on my tablet, and I maintain my various websites, edit videos, and do pretty much anything else that I need done from my tablet. If you are just using your device to browse the internet, send emails, or do some light photo or video editing, then you should consider lightening your load by replacing your laptop with a tablet. Plus, tablets nowadays have laptop-quality keyboards. And when you add the tablet's touch screen, it gives the tablet much more utility than lugging around the brick of a device that is a laptop for no good reason other than believing you're better off with a laptop. Most tablet producers will let you try it out for two weeks. I say take them up on their offer and experiment with only using the tablet for that time. You might be surprised by how much more efficient it is.

A backup charger

When on the go, the Spiritual Minimalist is prepared for adapting to change, including the unexpected change of not having a working outlet to charge up your devices. Many carry-on bags nowadays come with clunky charging ports embedded inside of the bag. I recommend skipping those and getting a portable charger. It's much smaller and more mobile, and you can replace it easily without needing to replace your entire carry-on.

...er and jumped at the chance.
I was first on the list. She time
...st sat and watched as hundreds
...gathered and checked in.
...I wasn't ready to go to France
...nd, the more uncomfortable
...would get bumped.
...fering a $500 coupon

...raw the plane
...They

Wednesday, Sunday

I woke up late and went down for b...
That's where I met Stephen. Stephen is...
Central Park West, he's been living in Pa...
for 18 years. He's married to a french woma...
teaches english to police officers, spea...
fast, takes short breaths before each sentence...
short, he makes listening to him a bit unc...
Apparently, he missed the plane, too, and p...
on volunteering at least until thursday w...
"absolutely" has to get back to Paris...
...akfast, he mentions many impressio...
...ences about his past and...
...an, Merrily, that also...
...her second night, and...
...together last nigh...
...together of them

PRINCIPLE 3:

No Throwaway Moments

"Everyone you meet has a divine gift for you.
Your job is to discover what that gift is."

—The Spiritual Minimalist

CHANCE ENCOUNTERS

"It's the best yoga class I've ever been to, and you have to come take it with me," my girlfriend April enthusiastically proclaimed. The year was 1998, long before everyone and their mother was teaching yoga. We were living in New York City—me on the Upper West Side and her on the Upper East Side of Manhattan. Sandwiched in between us was Central Park. And this amazing class of hers started at the height of rush hour on a weekday.

While I was a regular yoga practitioner, the thought of venturing across the park and to the Upper East Side for this class felt like a supreme waste of time. First of all, I enjoyed

my own teachers. Secondly, the commute from west to east would take three times longer than if I were going the other direction. So I resisted, put it off, and kept coming up with excuses. But she kept insisting, and one day I broke down and told her I was going to come to her (stupid) class.

When I arrived at the class five minutes late, all of the lights were off and the room was completely packed except for one empty yoga mat in the middle of a sea of silhouetted, deep-breathing yogis. I found my way to my mat and into Downward-Facing Dog, sensing something familiar about the experience though I couldn't place my finger on what it was.

As my eyes adjusted to the darkness, I was guided by the teacher to sync my breath with the rest of the class. He had an accent, and I guessed that he was either Australian or English.

"Inhale, exhale for one," he slowly commanded.

I noticed that his unhurried, hypnotic voice had a slight lisp.

"Inhale, exhale for two."

. . . but my shoulders were beginning to tire out.

"Inhale, exhale for three."

I could feel beads of sweat forming along my brow.

"Inhale, exhale for four."

My elbows were starting to buckle. *We need to hurry this along*, I thought.

"Inhale, exhale for five."

Okay, that's it. My arms are about to give out.

"Now bend your knees, and walk or hop your feet forward," he instructed.

Ah, relief.

The class went on like that, taking me to my physical and mental edge and then pulling me back more times than I could count. "This *is* a freaking good class," I thought to myself many times throughout. Now I understood why April wanted me to come here so badly. After the class, I thanked the teacher, whose name was Will, and left, never to return—purely due to its inconvenient time and location.

Four years later, my heart was nudging me to relocate from New York to Los Angeles and potentially start a new career as a yoga teacher. I was twenty-nine when I landed in West Hollywood, California, with a plan to take a yoga teacher training and figure things out from there. But before that, I needed to get the lay of the land. So I walked up the street to Crunch Fitness and requested a free pass to try out some of their yoga classes and get a feel for the West Coast style of yoga. They happily granted me a week-long pass along with a schedule of classes. I perused it and saw that there was a class the next morning at ten taught by Will (no last name).

A part of me wondered if it could be the same Will from New York, but what were the chances of that? Very slim. That next morning, I found myself in Downward-Facing Dog, and I heard that familiar accent. *Oh my God, I think it's the same Will!*

The problem was I never really saw his face in New York because it was so dark in the room—but I was almost certain it was him.

After the class, I went up to Will to thank him, and said, "I think we've met before. I came to your class in New York once, a few years ago." He cut me off, saying, "Yeah, I remember you. You're April's boyfriend."

"Ex-boyfriend," I corrected him. Good memory.

He said, "Yeah, I remember you because I had a bit of a crush on April, and I was disappointed when I discovered that she had a boyfriend." We both laughed.

Will had just moved to Los Angeles a couple of months before me. We bonded over the coincidence that we had both recently broken up with our girlfriends—circumstances that ironically led to us both leaving New York and relocating to Los Angeles.

Will and I began spending a lot of time together. We had so many shared interests: yoga, meditation, we both attended the same nondenominational spiritual center, we both liked to exercise daily, and we both ate most of our meals out. He became my yoga mentor. He got me into running. We met regularly for lunch. And Will became my meditation friend. Before we would go out to lunch, meet for a hike, or go to the movies, he would always ask me the dreaded four-word question: "Have you meditated yet?" And I would tell the truth—I hadn't.

The reason I dreaded that question was because, at the time, I found meditation so incredibly difficult and excruciatingly boring.

After all, I hadn't received any formal instruction, so I was just winging it each time I meditated. But Will seemed to be really into meditating, like all the time. And deep down, I knew it would be good for me to meditate on a more regular basis. So I would reluctantly agree to sit with my eyes closed and basically wait in agony for him to finish.

A few months later, Will mentioned that his meditation teacher was coming to Los Angeles from Arizona to give a presentation to some of his yoga students, and he invited me to come along. I agreed right away. I didn't even know Will had a meditation teacher. That explained why he enjoyed meditation so much. I was curious to meet this person who had taught him to be such an enthusiastic meditator.

The night came in February of 2003. It was a Sunday. I sat cross-legged on the floor of Will's apartment while the last few arrivals got settled. Then Will had us close our eyes, and a minute or two later, I heard a deep voice instruct us to open our eyes. And in the front of the room sat Will's meditation teacher: a short, clean-shaven white man with a receding hairline, dressed in khakis and a button-down shirt. Not what I was expecting a meditation guru to look like. Where's the robe? And the mala beads? And the long hair, and the accent? Furthermore, I hadn't heard him walk into the room—which was odd, because Will's floors were extra creaky. It was like he had floated out from the back room.

The teacher began talking about quantum physics, and the nature of the mind, and all the ways we've got the practice of meditation backwards: it wasn't a practice originally intended for monks, he carefully explained. It was for regular people—"householders," he called them. But when India was under attack by invaders many years ago, the monks became the "back-up discs" for meditation, preserving it. As a consequence, their austere lifestyle became synonymous with the practice of meditation.

I instantly took a liking to him, and my heart voice told me that he was meant to be my teacher.

While leaving the session that evening, I also knew that I was destined to become a meditation teacher—which was a revelation that I never would've imagined prior to attending that session. The problem was, there was no clear path to becoming a meditation teacher. My teacher kept referencing his Indian teacher, and I had no plans to go to India. So I just tucked that ambition into the back of my mind and began meditating with much more enjoyment. Now I understood why Will always wanted to meditate. It was fantastic once you knew what you were doing (see page 28 for basic meditation instructions). And I found myself waking up excited to sit on my couch for my morning practice.

Life continued on like that for about four years, until the opportunity I'd been waiting for presented itself: "Would

you like to travel to India with me and learn how to teach meditation?" my teacher asked.

It wasn't exactly an ideal time. I had just gotten involved in real estate in Los Angeles and was managing three properties on top of teaching my yoga classes. But I decided that I could potentially do both, so I jumped at the chance to join my teacher and some of his other protégés in India. I had no idea that I would lose all of my properties a year later—right after my training—when the real estate bubble burst, and that I would come within a hair of filing for bankruptcy.

But even though my credit was ruined, everything ended up working out. As it turned out, it was my foray into real estate that played a crucial role in my being able to pay for my meditation teacher training in the first place. Long story short, once I secured the zero-down-payment loans for my properties, I started receiving a slew of cash advance offers in the mail. My meditation teacher training tuition of $14,000 had to be paid in full in order for me to attend. Since I didn't have that kind of money with my meager yoga teacher's salary, I didn't know what I was going to do. So I just kept making plans to be at the training and trusted that it would somehow work out. And sure enough, a few days before the deadline, I received a cash advance offer in the mail for $14,000.

The offer said that I would have eighteen months to pay back the loan with zero interest. I knew that I was supposed to use it for my tuition. Once I completed my training and began teaching meditation a few months later, I was able to pay it off. Looking back, I now credit my real estate quagmire with putting me in a financial position to take the next step in following my heart voice.

Let's take this a step further, shall we? *You* reading this book was a result of my becoming a meditation teacher due to a chance encounter with my ex-girlfriend's former yoga teacher, whom I'd only met once in New York, in a class that I didn't even want to attend. And shortly after breaking up with said girlfriend, which prompted a move to Los Angeles, I bumped into that same yoga teacher, who happened to be teaching in my local gym, of which I was not a member.

Then we became friends, and a few months later, he invited me to his apartment to meet his former meditation teacher and my future guru—a man who'd recently retired after more than thirty years of teaching meditation and decided to un-retire just to teach Will's students, of which I was one. Cut to four years later (2007), I was on the brink of bankruptcy after having lost my shirt in real estate, yet I found myself flying off to India (thanks to that same terrible real estate experience) to train with the meditation teacher I met at my ex's former yoga teacher's apartment.

There were several other plot twists to the story, but the overall point is this: there is no linear path to our purpose.

Everything you've experienced in your life will come into play at some point. As you build up the courage to keep saying "yes" to your heart voice, one hundred times out of one hundred, no matter what it looks like on the surface, you will end up right where you're supposed to be, right when you're supposed to be there, even if it doesn't feel that way in the moment. Being a Spiritual Minimalist means that you give life the benefit of the doubt, and you trust that there are no throwaway moments.

THE GOOD PARTS

If and when you write about the story of your life, people who read it aren't going to want to hear about whatever wealth or influence you've received as much as they will want to hear about your hard times and your rock-bottom moments. They'll want to know about your breakdowns, your panic attacks, your dark-night-of-the-soul moments, and that time you had to live in your car.

They will want to know what adversity you had to overcome. The telling and retelling of your hardest and darkest moments, and of the leaps of faith you *had* to take in order to survive another day—those are the stories that will outlive you, get embellished, and continue to inspire future generations.

The bravery you are having to dig deep right now to find in order to follow your dreams will end up motivating someone who hears your story hundreds of years from now to keep going and not lose hope. *If you were able to do it*, they will think, *I know I can do it too.*

It's hard to see it sometimes, but today's struggles are not obstacles to your success, happiness, or life purpose. They are foundational to everything you are becoming and will become. And at some point in the near or distant future, they will be referred to as "the good parts" of your story.

One of my yoga teacher friend Will's traits that I haven't yet mentioned is how grateful he always was. He was by far the most grateful person I knew. When I would drop by Will's place, he would often greet me by saying, "Hit me with some gratitude, Brother Light." And then he and I would take turns listing off things we felt grateful for in that moment: our health, the beautiful Los Angeles weather, having nutritious food to eat, living in beautiful spaces, simple things like that.

I learned from Will to appreciate the often-overlooked in-between moments. And what I discovered is that if you take time to notice and appreciate the small things, then every day on Earth can feel like its own little miracle—and each moment contains a gift for you. It may be the gift of eyesight, or the gift of smell, or the gift of service. In other words, a conversation is never just a conversation. It is a chance to connect—to learn something of value from someone else's experience. Or a chance to offer a helping hand.

In 2020, while living in Bali, Will ended up having an adverse reaction to dengue fever that resulted in psychotic fits and paranoia. As a result, he became increasingly depressed and ended up taking his life. Due to the COVID-19 pandemic, I couldn't get into the country to help him. But thinking back to all of our interactions over the span of twenty years, it's the little things that I remember most fondly. I still today take a moment with whomever I'm around to recognize what I'm grateful for. In fact, Will was one of my main inspirations for going nomadic. He had gone nomadic about a year before me, after having a falling out with his landlord in the very apartment where I learned how to meditate.

Saying that there are no throwaway moments doesn't mean that there aren't bad things that happen. Through Will's example, I learned that even though bad things often happen, there's always something good that comes from it. And there's always something to be grateful for if we attune ourselves to notice it. As a Spiritual Minimalist, that's where you want to place the bulk of your attention—not on what's bad, but on what you're grateful for.

ACTION: GETTING INTO THE MOMENT

As a Spiritual Minimalist, being able to feel grateful in the most genuine way, especially when life gets tough, will become one of your most valuable assets. With practice, you will be able to anchor yourself in the moment by intentionally shifting your attention to whatever gifts or blessings you are surrounded by.

How to cultivate an ongoing attitude of gratitude:

Every morning, while lying in bed, you're going to spend the first few minutes upon awakening by placing your attention on five things that you're grateful for. That's it. You don't have to write anything down (unless you want to). Just ask yourself, What's good about this moment? The answers can be as simple as:

1. I'm grateful that I woke up.
2. I'm grateful that I feel rested.
3. I'm grateful to have a job.
4. I'm grateful for my strength.
5. I'm grateful for my family.

Then, throughout your day, especially if you're feeling bothered by something or someone, keep repeating that exercise. List another five simple things that you're grateful for. See each one in your mind's eye before moving on to the next one. And you will notice an immediate boost in your energy, in your ability to be present, and in your appreciation for that moment.

It is from this space that you will be able to more easily source inspiration, connection, creative solutions, and even *more* gratitude for everything you're experiencing, knowing that it is constantly leading you to opportunities for expansion.

A Spiritual Minimalist tries to remain in a state of gratitude as much as possible. In fact, you could go so far as to say that the concept of Spiritual Minimalism is synonymous with gratitude—meaning, you are a Spiritual Minimalist to the extent that you can find gratitude in any given moment. And for that reason, there's no such thing as an ungrateful Spiritual Minimalist.

THE BLESSING-CURSE PREMISE

Have you ever found yourself wondering whether something you're experiencing is a blessing or a curse? If you're only assessing the situation from a surface-level perspective of cause and effect, it can be hard to tell.

Think of it like this: for something to truly be a curse, it would have to place you in a negative position forever—like going to eternal hell. In other words, if everlasting hell exists, there's no coming back from that.

But if you don't believe in eternal hell, then that means everything you experience—even the so-called "bad" stuff—must somehow, and in some way, be a blessing (albeit sometimes a blessing in disguise), because at the very least it may be leading to expansion of your awareness, or soul growth.

Let's suppose you recently got fired. Now, getting fired would be the surface-level interpretation of what happened, based on the fact that you lost your job. But you've also been handed a divine opportunity to pivot, to learn, and to find comfort in the unknown. And with this level of freedom, you may be ready to take a leap of faith in the direction of your passion—something you wouldn't have seriously considered back when you were in a more comfortable yet uninspired work situation.

Maybe you got dumped? Or you could see it as you being liberated from a relationship that was either no longer serving your "soul" goals or you were no longer serving your partner's soul goals.

You lost a close friend or relative? As awful as this can feel, there is a possibility that their soul had a contract with your soul to help you learn about loss and love (again, soul goals) through death, and it's likely that you've helped them in that same way in a past lifetime.

You don't like the politician who recently got elected? He or she is your catalyst to get more informed, to become more involved, and to be the change that you want to see in your part of the world.

So you see, the next time something "bad" happens and you wonder if it was a blessing or a curse, the Spiritual Minimalist way of looking at it is to opt to see it as a blessing each time, and then work backward from there to find supporting evidence.

By all means, you can have your mourning period, but try to remember that there's immense power in reconciling for yourself how and why you have been gifted this blessing and acting from that greater sense of purpose.

Now it's your turn: take a situation you're currently experiencing and reframe it by imagining how it could be happening *for* you instead of *to* you, or how it can help you help someone else, or how it can potentially lead you closer to your purpose.

WHAT'S IN MY BAG: WATER

Most people feel that they should be drinking more water, and we all know that plastic water bottles are terrible for the environment. Therefore, you may want to consider adding a reusable water bottle to your Spiritual Minimalism kit. If you've never used a reusable water bottle, you may be thinking, "A few ie lobby.

Now, this is going to sound unbelievable, bu
a sample from my short life of just ho
all the world is:

I'm sitting in Ph One, and this tall, st
d jovial black man is in there speaking
ent English and he starts to look at me
ats your name?" he asked me curiously.
n you before, somewhere." I told him n
ry and he interrupted, "You're from Chica
amed. I saw you in Elite's book. I ha
te." Apparently, Earnest moved to Paris
ars ago, he is a photographer, that tests al
clusively with Ph One and he met my b
ny, over the summer in Chicago, were s
dly refused his services. He immedia
gan asking me about my Paris agenda an
ering me advice. It was great. Then, he.
t he heard of a casting he wanted me to g
e left and went next door to Absolut wo
ency and came back with Christian,
ker for Absolut. Christian told me.
ld send me on the casting and left. Wh
iting Earnest got impatient and wante
t be me to Absolut to get the booking from C

plastic bottles here and there isn't hurting the environment." But what if millions or billions of other people thought that way? Next thing you know, there are enough plastic water bottles used in the United States each year to encircle the Earth 150 times when laid end to end. That's our current situation. And it takes each one about 500 years to decompose. So a reusable water bottle is the best solution to staying hydrated.

For relatively healthy people who are not taking water-retaining medications, the recommended amount of daily water consumption is about six cups a day. And like the majority of the items in my bag, these six cups of water can serve multiple functions.

It's nature's moisturizer

Humans are seventy-five percent water, so not drinking enough water will leave you dehydrated and dry whereas drinking a sufficient amount of water hydrates you and keeps your skin looking healthier.

It can substitute for mouthwash

Did you know that conventional mouthwash is bad for your microbiome, and that it's as effective to swish some water in your mouth after brushing?

It keeps your teeth white(r)

If you drink coffee, tea, or wine, make sure to swish some fresh water around your mouth to keep your teeth bright.

It's nature's aspirin

If you're coming down with a headache, make sure you're not just dehydrated by drinking a cup or two of water.

It will hold you over until your next meal

If you're "starving" but you're not going to have food for a while, drink a cup of water and you'll be able to go a little longer without getting hangry. And when you do get around to eating, water helps with digestion and prevents constipation.

I've found that a good twenty-four-ounce refillable water bottle is large enough to meet your daily water needs but small enough to fit into an average-size cup holder—and six cups equals two bottles of water.

If you want to get very systematic with it, you can drink one twenty-four-ounce bottle of water in the first half of the day and one more bottle of water in the second half of the day, and you've met the daily recommendation of six cups. Of course, if you are not sure about the right amount of water for you, check with your doctor. But any doctor will agree that you should be drinking more water than you're drinking sugary, alcoholic, or packaged beverages like kombucha or iced coffee.

PRINCIPLE 4:

Give What You Want

"We don't create abundance.
Abundance is already there. We either
create access or limitations to it."

—The Spiritual Minimalist

NO FREE LUNCH

Ever wonder why complimentary "bar food" like nuts, pretzels, olives, and popcorn are generally salty in nature? Turns out the trend of making salty snacks available to bar patrons didn't exactly originate from the altruistic nature of bar owners. In the late nineteenth century, American saloon owners with low foot traffic came up with a clever ploy to entice potential customers to come in and purchase at least one beer: they advertised a "free" lunch, mainly consisting of snacks that induced thirst, including salty nuts, pretzels, olives, and popcorn.

The thinking was, after a hungry patron wolfed down a couple of handfuls of free nuts and pretzels, they would become so parched that they would have to order a cold beer to wash it down. And, hopefully, they would order a few more beers as they kept munching away.

What the patron didn't know was that the saloon owners charged a premium for the same beers patrons could've ordered at a neighboring saloon for less. Then again, the saloons down the street didn't offer a free "lunch."

The ploy worked like a charm—that is, until customers caught on to the clever scheme and word began to spread that the free lunch offer was actually a bait and switch, since they were being charged more for their drinks. And thus, a truism was born—one that would continue to spread for generations: "There's no such thing as a *free* lunch."

That saying has transcended bar snacks and now applies to any offer that sounds too good to be true. And from the Spiritual Minimalist perspective, *nothing* of true value comes without a direct (or indirect) cost. In other words, you get back in direct proportion to what you give.

DETERMINE YOUR OWN VALUE

There's nothing wrong with someone advertising their product or service for free, so long as you understand that there is no such thing as free. As you embody that understanding, not only can you adjust your expectations accordingly, but you can have some fun with it. You can determine your own value on the front end instead of being assigned a value on the back end—because you're not afraid of there being a cost.

In fact, you already know that there's a cost. And to expect to get something of quality for little to no exchange is not only naive, it's also delusional. It doesn't matter what the offering looks like at face value. *There is no such thing as a free lunch.*

As a Spiritual Minimalist, you want to engage in all relationships with full awareness that there is *always* an exchange, whether it's obvious or not. And if you can't see or understand the exchange clearly, you're happy to create one for yourself. It doesn't have to be money. It could be your attention. It could be recognition. It could be gratitude. Or, you could be doing a good deed to make it a karmic exchange.

The important thing is to think in terms of exchange, and to remember that free often means expensive on the back end—in the form of a conversation you may not want to have, a favor you're not going to want to return, a sales pitch you're not interested in, time you weren't prepared to give, or an amount of money that you feel is too much for whatever they offered in exchange.

As a Spiritual Minimalist, you prefer to make clean and clear exchanges, which means knowing the right questions to ask on the front end—not in a skeptical or cynical way, but in a curious and enthusiastic way. For example, if someone offers you a place to crash for the weekend, there may be an unspoken expectation for you to help clean or cook or run household errands while you're staying there. Or you may be expected to be overly gracious and thankful. Or you could be expected to have long conversations with your host about their relationship woes. *There's always an exchange.* When you understand what it is, you may decide that it's actually less expensive to pay for a hotel room, depending on how much work you have to do or on how much you value your privacy.

If you wait to figure out the exchange on the back end, at the behest of the proprietor or the friend offering you a place to crash, you could find yourself in a tricky situation where you are giving much more than you're receiving in return— you're overpaying for beer to help, or you're up until the wee hours of the morning giving free advice that your friend is most likely going to ignore.

You could also be compromising your peace of mind with these nonsensical conversations which, in turn, causes you to lose sleep. And what's the cost of being tired the next day because you didn't sleep well the night before, after putting yourself into a situation where you supposedly saved $50 by not having to get a hotel room, but you were up all night giving advice that will likely be ignored? Did you really save $50, or did you just pay $500 for the mistake-prone, poor-quality decision-making you'll likely suffer the next day due to missed sleep?

I know of a friend of a friend who is always trying to save money on flights. Instead of paying the extra $80 for a two-hour direct flight, he will opt for a ten-hour connecting flight to the same destination, thinking that he's saving money but not realizing that he's going to spend more money in time wasted sitting around in the airport for hours on end waiting for the connecting flight, while snacking on expensive yet low-quality food, drinking high-priced water, and being unproductive. Or, if he booked a red-eye, he essentially loses a night of sleep to save money—which means every decision he makes over those next few sleep-deprived days will be compromised.

What is the true cost of spending an extra eight hours in transit? What is the value of a night of sleep? How much is a good decision worth versus a sleep-deprived decision? There is no free lunch.

A big part of practicing Spiritual Minimalism is learning to recognize the value of how you're spending your time, to make sure it aligns with your overall priorities—and we're not just talking about physical costs, but also energetic and karmic costs. There is a steep cost to taking a red-eye flight (on top of whatever the advertised cost is). There is a cost to being frugal as opposed to spending for quality or functionality. There's even a cost to not speaking your truth, a cost to not exercising, and a cost to taking a so-called shortcut. There's a steep cost to breaking a promise, as well as a cost to not following through on a habit (the cost of starting over), a cost to being stingy, and a cost to gossiping. Everything has a cost.

Therefore, it's advantageous to either understand what those costs are, or, when possible, to negotiate those costs up front by suggesting your payment preemptively.

This concept of the exchange will play a key role in your journey as a Spiritual Minimalist, and understanding it will take shape in several ways. It will inspire you to lead with generosity, to ask different questions, and to consider all sides in order to make sure any exchange feels like a win-win. If someone senses that they're losing, that's going to have a long-term cost. So you need to make sure that the exchange feels mutually beneficial.

Something else to consider: as a Spiritual Minimalist, you're never just making an exchange with an individual. Your tab is ultimately being managed by "the Universe." And while an individual or an organization is sometimes the beneficiary of your exchange, *you* are the actual beneficiary. When you pull the lens back far enough, the Spiritual Minimalist understands that you're only ever giving back to yourself. So being cheap with someone is, in actuality, you being cheap with yourself. Shortchanging someone is really just shortchanging yourself. In other words, you are never *not* engaged in an exchange. Every relationship is ultimately an exchange between you and you. And because as a Spiritual Minimalist you will begin to understand this better than most, you will avoid the unnecessarily costly free-lunch trap.

THE ESSENCE OF DISCIPLINE

Here's how I define discipline: it's taking short-term actions for results you desire over the long term. As anyone who's tried to be disciplined knows, you're rarely going to be inspired to be disciplined because discipline requires delayed gratification. And few people have the self-control to delay gratification, including Spiritual Minimalists. But what the Spiritual Minimalist does have is the ability and willingness to look at the truth of the situation and put the necessary stopgaps in place.

Here's an example to clarify what I mean. When I was writing my first book, a self-published book called *The Inner Gym*, I wanted to have it published by a certain date. Yet I had been dragging my feet with it for nearly four years, so there was nothing in my past that indicated I was going to finish by the date I had in mind. I got to the point where I was tired of lying to myself about when I was going to finish writing the book. I knew deep down that I was just going to come up with another really important excuse about why I couldn't finish it by that date, and I'd pick another date, and then another date, and keep kicking the can down the road.

So one day, after getting fed up with my own lies, I decided to write a check for $4,000, which was an amount I had in the bank but that I couldn't afford to lose. I wrote the check to a friend who didn't need the money, and I made a contract between us saying that if I didn't finish my manuscript by a specific date, he was obligated to cash the $4,000 check and use the money for anything that didn't involve me. We both signed the contract.

After that, I had no problems finishing my manuscript. I didn't even need discipline. I happily made the time and even finished a week in advance, just in case anything unexpected happened so I didn't risk losing my money. That was when I discovered the secret to discipline: it's never about discipline—it's about honesty. I made myself honest by putting something that was meaningful to me on the line. As soon as I did that, I found the discipline. In other words, you are only disciplined to the extent that you are telling yourself the truth.

As a Spiritual Minimalist, if you are able to admit to yourself that you are not going to wake up at six every morning to work on your passion project, no matter how good your intentions are, because you've never done so consistently, maybe you need to put some money on the line. Or maybe you need to make a contract between yourself and someone else to hold you accountable—whichever one motivates you to be the most honest with yourself about what you want to do.

If you have a real conversation with yourself and actually put something on the line that you cannot back out of or afford to lose, then I guarantee you that the discipline you're after won't even be necessary. And you'll learn what it takes to truly follow through on your word.

The best part is that once you implement this strategy with one thing, you can confidently use it for anything you feel inspired to change in your life. And as a Spiritual Minimalist, you prove that change is indeed possible.

ACTION: LEAVE NO TRASH BEHIND

I heard an interview with Clemson University football coach Dabo Swinney, who talked about how one of the rules of his football team was to leave no trash behind. Literally, every locker room they walked out of needed to be spotless. There would be no trash left on their bus for the bus driver to clean up. And after leaving the movie theater on Friday nights, they were to leave it cleaner than it was when they arrived there.

Coach Swinney said that one of his proudest moments as a coach was when he received a letter from the University of Notre Dame after a game that Clemson lost in double overtime. The letter said that Notre Dame had never had a visiting team leave the locker room so clean. Coach Swinney beamed with pride, because even after a devastating defeat, his team held up the standard that they agreed upon at the beginning of the year, by leaving that locker room better than they found it. If you want excellence, you must give excellence, even when you don't feel like it . . . *especially* when you don't feel like it.

To embody this principle of giving what you want to receive, your Spiritual Minimalism practice is to leave all spaces better than you found them, even when you're not in the mood or when it's inconvenient to do so. This means that when you visit a public bathroom, when you go to a movie, when you ride in an Uber, or when you're visiting someone's home, pick up after yourself, clean up any trash left behind by others, and leave the space beautiful. In other words, treat every space like it's your own—as if your personal hero is going to use the space right after you. It doesn't matter how everyone else is treating the space. Maybe no one has led by example, and now it's your opportunity to show what it looks like when someone cares enough to treat a common space in an uncommon way. Plus, you never know who's paying attention.

A CURE FOR LONELINESS

In my experience, when you stop drinking, you eventually lose the desire to be around people who are drinking heavily. Yet much of our socializing as adults is geared around alcohol consumption—which means that for a long time, I wasn't really going out.

I wouldn't say I was necessarily lonely, but I was definitely lonesome, and I was single. So, in 2014, I decided to create what I felt was missing: an alcohol-free social event that was geared around inspiration.

I started by asking myself, What do I like? I like live music, I like TED talks. I like stand-up comedy. I like philanthropy. So I combined all of those elements into a ninety-minute social event. I rented a dance studio in West L.A. for $50 and called my event The Shine.

I sent out an email to some of my friends, and we ended up getting about ten or twelve people at the first Shine event. I continued hosting them once a week, paying for it out of my pocket. Then we began collecting donations at the end and giving all of the money to charity.

Next thing you know, we were getting 100, then 200, then 300 people coming to these events. And then they're happening in New York, and then London. And it becomes a whole thing. The *New York Times* profiled it, along with NBC, ABC, and other major media outlets.

They covered it because it was an alcohol-free event for adults on a Saturday night, and there was nothing else like it happening at the time. The press we got was all organic. We didn't have a PR person. It was all a result of consistency and word of mouth.

I ended up creating what I felt was lacking. I never made a dime off of it directly, although I landed my first book deal after it was covered in the *Times*. But The Shine was completely run by volunteers for the five years it existed.

Aside from my day job of teaching meditation, The Shine gave me something else to work toward—something that provided me with a paycheck for my soul, because it brought people together around inspiration and created a lot of amazing memories in the process. I even met my girlfriend through The Shine. She was inspired to volunteer, and we connected that way. So I ended up getting *everything* that I wanted when I was lonely by focusing not on what I was lacking, but on what I could give.

My advice to you, as a practicing Spiritual Minimalist, is this: if you feel you're lacking something, focus on how you can give it. For instance, if you don't feel connected to the people or events around you, create the event that you fantasize about attending. I guarantee you, if you're creating it from the right place and everything is authentic, people who share your values will come to your event, and you will create community around it.

Creating community is one of the best ways to eradicate loneliness. You displace it by focusing on giving. And it doesn't have to be some elaborate event. It could just be a hiking group. Or it could be a game night. It could be a dinner night if you like preparing home-cooked meals. Everybody loves home-cooked food. So invite a few of your friends to come around and enjoy some of your cooking.

I used to do that, too. I had a small gathering called The Community Table where, every Monday night, I would invite six people to come to my apartment and enjoy a three-course meal prepared by me or a friend. It was wonderful. The Community Table lasted about a year and a half, and I met dozens of fascinating people over deliciously prepared meals and created many lasting memories. Before that, I hosted a dinner and game night every Thursday at the West Hollywood apartment where I first started teaching meditation. Find your version of that. As a Spiritual Minimalist, don't wait for people to invite you to gatherings. Get into the habit of creating what it is that you want to see and experience, and you will displace loneliness with inspiration.

WHAT'S IN MY BAG: THANK-YOU NOTES

One item I always carry in my bag is some type of paper—either in the form of a notepad, a journal, or loose sheets of note paper. Why? Because you never know when you'll be inspired to leave a note of gratitude.

In our digitized world, one of the kindest, sweetest, and most unexpected tokens of appreciation is to take the time to hand-write someone a thank-you note. And in order to do so, you always want to have something to write with and something to write on. There are numerous reasons why you should always have something physical to write on. Here are the multiple uses of your notepad:

Thank-you notes

Find a notepad with pages that you can remove with relative ease. The cleaner the edge, the better, as it reflects your cleanliness as a Spiritual Minimalist. You should have a wide-tip pen or retractable pencil to jot notes. If you can study calligraphy, that's even better. At the very least, practice your penmanship so your notes are legible. Leaving a note is only valuable if it can be read (and even shared) with ease. I like to take a photo of my notes to record what I wrote in case I want to reference it at a later date. You never know where these notes will end up . . . perhaps in a museum 200 years from now.

Journal

If you are an aspiring writer or recorder of your personal history, then a journal is an invaluable resource. I haven't been as consistent with my journaling as I would like to be. But when I have journaled, I've never regretted it, and I thoroughly enjoy going back and reflecting on my past experiences, especially when I get ready to write about them. Of course, you can type your journal into your device, but hand-writing your thoughts has its place as well. It's really just a matter of personal preference. If space is an issue, after filling up one journal, I suggest taking a photo of each page, then discarding it before starting the next one.

Origami

Have you learned any basic origami? If not, you should. I learned how to fold paper into the shape of a crane, and now I can leave a paper crane as a small token of appreciation for anyone I wish. There's obviously a slight learning curve, but once you memorize the sequence of folds, you'll find it very meditative. And the effect that it has well exceeds the effort that it takes to learn and the few minutes it takes to make one.

Notepad

How many times do we hear names that are hard to pronounce? Writing them down phonetically is an excellent way to remember them. As Dale Carnegie reminds us in his human behavior bible, *How to Win Friends and Influence People*, the sweetest sound in any language is the sound of a person's name (pronounced correctly). Your handy notepad will ensure that you are the one person to meet someone with a complicated name and actually remember it—because you took the time and care to write it down and study it. Doing this puts you in the top one percent of people.

Flirting

My friend Will used to call his flirtatious hand-written note cards "boomerangs." It works like this: you write down your message, for example, "Hi, I love your style. And I'm not sure if you're available, but if so, I'd love to meet you for a coffee sometime. My number is xxx-xxxx.—Will (the handsome guy from Heart Cafe)." Then you fold it and hand it to the person who has your attention. And you go about your business. And usually, if the person is indeed interested and available, they will respond, either by accepting your invitation via text or politely declining your invitation if they are not available. But either way, because you put a little effort into your presentation, you will usually get a message back—hence "boomerang."

PRINCIPLE 5:

Follow Curiosity

"Don't worry about finding your
purpose. Just follow your curiosity
and your purpose will find you."

—The Spiritual Minimalist

WHEN A SEED IS PLANTED

When I went nomadic in 2018, it actually wasn't the first time
I'd done something like that. It was the third. The first time I
went nomadic was after college. I landed a job at a boutique
advertising agency in Chicago. After a few months, I decided
to quit and try modeling. I'd done a few rinky-dink fashion
shows in college; at one show, I overheard a couple of guys
talking about how South Beach, Florida, was turning into an
emerging fashion scene—and a seed was planted in my heart
to one day relocate to South Florida and pursue modeling.

I informed my creative director that I was going to be leaving the agency and wasn't sure what my next step would be, though secretly my heart voice was persuading me to give modeling a shot. My creative director wished me well, and I spent the next few weeks looking for representation at Chicago modeling agencies.

I got some pictures taken with a photographer friend of mine and shopped them around to some open calls—and all of the agents rejected me. A week or so later, while in a cafe, I struck up a conversation with a local fashion photographer and told her how I was rejected by all of the agencies. She asked to see my photos, and after I showed her, she explained to me that they were too artistic, that what I really needed were fashion photos—so she offered to shoot some for me. I accepted and then went back around to all of the agencies with my new photos, and I got rejected by everyone again—except the last agency I visited. The agent, Amy, agreed to represent me.

Although I was pleased, I informed Amy on my first day with the agency that I was planning to go to South Beach, and she suggested that I stay in Chicago for the summer to get some more photos taken, which I agreed to do. And one day in July I got a call from Amy requesting that I come meet a Parisian modeling agent named Paul, who was in town from the top agency in Paris, PH One.

I arrived, and after waiting for a bit, I got to meet with Paul. He spoke with a thick French accent and greeted me warmly, pronouncing his name as "Pool." I handed Pool my portfolio and stared at him while he flipped through each page, studying my photos. Finally, he handed it back to me and said, "You would do well in Paris."

That really made my day. After getting rejected by all of the Chicago agencies twice, I was now finally being validated by one of the top agents in one of the biggest fashion markets in the world. So when Pool said I would do well in Paris, what I heard him say was, "You should come to Paris, and you'll be a star."

What I didn't realize at the time (because I didn't have enough experience in the industry yet) was that if Pool truly thought I would do well in Paris, he would've offered to represent me on the spot, possibly even flying me over and putting me up in a model's apartment. But that's not what happened. I met with him for a couple of minutes, and that was it. "You would do well" was a pleasantry that he probably told every model who met with him that day, just to be cordial.

But now the idea of going to Paris was planted in my heart, along with South Beach. I figured I would go to Florida first, and then I would travel to see Pool and join his Parisian agency. It was all set.

That October, I left Chicago for South Beach, and I got rejected by all of the agencies there, except for the last one.

I got more photos for my portfolio, and I booked maybe three or four jobs in the span of six months. After South Beach, I traveled to New York City to find representation . . . and I got rejected by all of the major agencies there. And I returned to Chicago. I decided that while it wasn't happening for me in the States, maybe it was time to head over to see Pool in Paris. At that point I was so used to rejection that I figured I had nothing to lose.

With the last of my money, I booked a one-way flight from Chicago to Paris, connecting through Newark. And when I arrived at the connecting gate, the gate agent announced that the flight to Paris was oversold. Since Pool had no idea that I was even coming, I decided to give up my seat in exchange for the $500 flight voucher they were offering to volunteers, and they rebooked me on a flight the next evening.

I showed up the following night and it was the same song, second verse: an oversold flight. They needed volunteers to give up their seat. I gave up mine and was awarded another $500 flight voucher. I figured if the modeling thing didn't work out, I could do this for a living.

I returned the next night, and again it was the same deal. I gave up my seat, but they ended up having one seat left on the flight. So next thing I knew, I was enroute to Paris with more than enough money in flight vouchers to book a return flight in case things didn't work out with Pool.

When I arrived the next morning, I went to check into a hostel, but it was only 9 am, and check-in wasn't until 3 pm. So I took my belongings with me to Pool's agency, PH One.

To my mild disappointment, they informed me that Pool wasn't in town. But the receptionist asked to see my portfolio. Then she disappeared into the back and returned not even a minute later to let me know that they already had a model who looked like me, and that I should see other agencies. Rejected but not dejected, I sat in the lobby and began scanning a list of local agencies to see who I wanted to be rejected by next.

Meanwhile, a tall, heavyset Black guy was on the other side of the lobby conversing in French with two models. And every now and again he would glance over in my direction. I wasn't sure why he was looking at me, but I was hoping he wouldn't come over and start speaking to me in French because I had long forgotten the few phrases I memorized in my college French class.

When he walked over, to my surprise he greeted me in perfect American English.

"Hey, are you from Chicago?" he asked.

"Well, I'm not from there, but I was just living there."

"I'm from Chicago, and I'm a photographer. I remember seeing your composite card at one of the agencies, and I never forget a face."

"Really?! Wow, what a coincidence."

"My name is Ernest," he said, extending his hand.

"Nice to meet you, Ernest."

"So what happened here? Did they sign you?"

"No, they told me they had someone who looked like me, and to try other agencies."

"Hmmm, okay. I want you to come with me."

"Sure."

Ernest led me out into the hallway. We walked down the hall to the adjacent office, which had a sign that read "Crystal." It was another modeling agency, I assumed. As we entered, I saw a young model standing with her back to the door. She turned around, noticed me, and called my name.

"Oh my God, what are you doing here?!"

"I just got to Paris! What are *you* doing here?"

"I've been here modeling for a year," she said.

Her name was Lauriel, and she happened to be in that rinky-dink fashion show with me in college, back when I first heard about the fashion scene in South Beach. And now here we were in Paris. She was with a French-American friend of hers, Jeffery. After they found out that I didn't have a place to stay, Jeffery said his mom had just left town for a few months to visit his sister and offered her apartment to me for next to nothing. It was located in the 18th arrondissement, one of the most charming districts in all of Paris, facing the historical

Sacré-Cœur church. Plus, Ernest's agent friend at Crystal offered to send me out on model castings.

So, after two delayed flights, a botched check-in at a hostel, and a rejection from Pool's agency, I ended up having everything I needed within a couple of hours of landing in Paris—all from following my curiosity.

I stayed in Paris for about six months connecting with a wonderful group of friends, and I eventually got signed by one of the top agencies there. Later, I met the top agent in New York while he was in Paris, and he brought me to New York to begin modeling there. And while my modeling career didn't start the traditional way, I continued to follow my curiosity. I ended up working with agents and having adventures that were more amazing than anything I imagined for myself. And New York happened to be the place where I was first introduced to meditation.

The moral of this story is, when a seed is planted in your heart, as a Spiritual Minimalist you have to take it seriously, because that seed is pointing you to the next step along your path. And you never have to know what your purpose is. All you have to do is keep following your curiosity, and your purpose will eventually find you.

A HOP OF FAITH

In 2020 I started a podcast that featured the stories of people who had found their purpose. After conducting around 200 in-depth interviews with ordinary people who took extraordinary leaps of faith to find their purpose, here's what I deduced.

There are two motivating factors for taking a leap of faith. The first one is pain. We find ourselves in situations that are so unbearable, so intolerable, that the idea of remaining in them is no longer an option. I call this the burning-building motivation for leaping into your purpose. In other words, it's too hot to remain in the status quo, and you have no choice but to take the leap.

The other approach is curiosity. A thought or an idea gets planted in your consciousness, and it won't go away. No matter how much you try to ignore it, it keeps bugging you, during the day and into the night. It lingers in the back of your mind. It keeps coming up in conversations. You start seeing mentions of it in movies, in magazines, and on billboards. It becomes the subject of many of your daydreams. Eventually, you take it seriously enough to act upon it. And the deeper you explore it, the more fascinated you become by it.

There is a third reason why some people follow their purpose: they didn't have a choice. But we'll talk more about this path when going over the final principle of Spiritual Minimalism, which is the freedom of choicelessness.

When it comes to corruption, they say follow the money, and it will lead you to the source of the corruption. Well, when it comes to finding your purpose, like my podcast guests experienced, you must follow your curiosity—no matter how strange it sounds, no matter how many people laugh at you, no matter how unqualified you may feel to explore the area that you're curious about. Just keep following it, and it will eventually lead you to your purpose.

When I went to Paris, it was my first time taking a major leap of faith in the direction of my purpose. But if you go back and reread that story, you'll see that I had been hopping around—from my advertising job to modeling, then from Chicago to Miami, then to New York, then back to Chicago and over to Paris, and finally back to New York. So in truth, the Paris "leap" that became this story of amazing serendipity was just another hop in a series of smaller hops.

When you hear about someone taking a big leap of faith, rarely does it mean they got a wave of inspiration and the next day quit their job and made a stark change in their life. It's more likely that they started with a series of baby hops.

Before my most recent nomadic adventure (the one I'm currently on as I write this book), I was curious to see how few items I really needed when nomading, so I experimented with packing fewer and fewer items each time I went out of town for work trips before I finally took the plunge and got rid of everything. So although it looks like I dramatically changed my entire life overnight, the reality is I had already experimented dozens of times with what I would need while on the road, and how to get by on less, *before* I leapt into action.

In fact, when you closely examine the life of anyone who has made an extreme change, you will almost always find a trail of baby hops. You'll see how they toyed with the idea for a while, then practiced it in small, manageable ways, building confidence while working out the kinks. Then, after much practice, they took the leap. But by that time, the leap felt much less scary and more like the next step in the evolution of their purpose.

Whatever stark changes you want to make now, start by taking baby hops. And when you finally go all in, everyone will see it as a scary leap of faith—but since you followed your curiosity, you'll just see it as the next step in a progression of dozens, if not hundreds, of steps. And with each hop of faith, you will get closer and closer to your purpose.

ACTION: FLANEUR-ING

For Spiritual Minimalists, walking isn't just walking. Walking can also be a productive time for observing, for practicing mindfulness, for brainstorming and iterating on an idea, for

taking a meeting, for taking a break, for returning a phone call, or for catching up on a podcast or audiobook.

If you're looking for a good reason to take a walk, it's not hard to find one. Or you can just walk for the sake of walking, which is known as flaneur-ing—the art of aimless walking. Yes, it's an art. Flaneur-ing was first written about in the late nineteenth century in Paris, as men and women of leisure would intentionally walk around at a casual pace with no specific destination in mind. The idea was to wander, people watch, observe the environment, to get "lost"—and in the process, to discover something new and interesting either about the environment or about the flaneur's relationship to the environment. In essence, a flaneur follows their curiosity.

Flaneur-ing was typically practiced alone, as one was more prone to observe one's surroundings when not distracted by a companion. And it was also done sober, as there is a natural high from being so completely immersed in the experience that you wouldn't want to ruin with alcohol or other consciousness-altering substances.

Many of the Paris-based impressionist painters were said to be flaneurs. They would wander around the city, following their natural curiosity, getting lost, stumbling upon some impressive perspective of a landscape or an interesting way that light danced along the contours of an object, and they would paint it—hence the term "impressionist."

The Spiritual Minimalist is a modern-day flaneur who enjoys roaming around on foot, sometimes with a clear destination in mind, but often just for the sake of moving their body—*always* allowing curiosity to dictate the path.

We also know that movement is healthy. And daily walking is the best way to facilitate regular movement. The flaneurs may not have realized the extent of the advantages one gets from walking every day, but here's how modern medicine says we benefit from making walking a daily priority:

- Walking prevents dementia and reduces the chances of getting Alzheimer's disease.
- It releases endorphins, which reduce stress.
- Moving your legs improves your eyesight.
- The exercise provided by walking prevents heart disease and reduces your chances of lung disease.
- A daily half-hour walk lowers cholesterol.
- Walking improves digestion and regulates bowel movements.
- It has been said that 10,000 steps a day is as effective as a full workout.
- Walking leads to sturdier muscles and reduces inflammation in the joints.
- It relieves back pain and improves posture.
- Walking improves depression symptoms and helps to calm the mind.

The Spiritual Minimalist walks ideally several thousand steps a day. One mile is 2,000 steps (one kilometer is about 1,400 steps), and it typically takes about twenty to twenty-five minutes to walk one mile at a leisurely pace. So you can hit a goal of 6,000 steps within about an hour of walking each day. This can include the steps you take while walking around your house.

If you have the option to take the stairs, you can add to your steps. And you can start looking at your errands as opportunities to get in more steps. Usually, we feel lucky if we score a parking space close to the entrance of wherever we're going. But the Spiritual Minimalist considers themselves lucky if they park far enough away to get in some extra steps.

So start taking advantage of the best and most sustainable exercise we can get each day, which is plain old walking. Become a modern-day flaneur. You don't need a reason to go for a stroll. Lace up your shoes and just allow inspiration to guide you. See what you can see. Aim for at least 6,000 steps today, and over time, see if you can work your way up to 10,000 steps. You can easily track your steps with a smartphone or a smart watch.

Be warned: it's addictive. And once you get into the habit of walking, you won't want to stop, as it is the optimal way to calm the mind while exercising the body and getting more familiar with your neighborhood. You will also give yourself an opportunity to literally follow your curiosity.

WHAT'S IN MY BAG: THE WHITE SHOE

The go-to pair of shoes for a Spiritual Minimalist is a basic white casual sneaker, preferably leather (or faux leather). I've tried several pairs over the years, and I'm not loyal to any one brand. However, I typically avoid canvas shoes because, when it comes to taking care of what you have, white leather shoes are the easiest to keep clean.

All you need to do is wipe them down with a rag or a wet wipe every couple of days before you head out, and if you stay on top of it, the white really pops. It's a classy look that can be easily dressed up or down, depending on the occasion.

Also, they're easy to find because just about every designer makes their own version of an all-white casual shoe. You can find them in high-top, if that's more your vibe, or low-top (which is my personal preference).

A couple of tricks for keeping your shoes looking new:

Wiping: Wipe your shoes down every few days. This does not have to be an elaborate process. If you have a hand towel or a rag, just wet it in water and wipe down your shoe. If you're really strapped for time, you can use a wet wipe to clean your white shoes.

Laces: Either clean your laces or buy a new pair of white laces from any shoe store or drugstore. And once you wipe down the leather and re-lace them, they will look brand new.

Socks: It's important to keep the inside of your shoes as fresh as possible. Sock-wise, I wear black, no-show socks because it's easier to keep black socks looking clean, and you're not going to see them anyway. Plus, you need socks because the last thing you want is to be stinking up someone's place with smelly shoes and feet. So *always* wear socks.

PRINCIPLE 6:

Find Comfort in Discomfort

"Everyone living at the edge of their comfort
zone has impostor syndrome. If you don't
have impostor syndrome, go further."

—The Spiritual Minimalist

THE STIFFEST YOGI

I moved to Los Angeles in 2002 with a vision of teaching the
style of yoga that I had been practicing for several years, which
was *Vinyasa* flow.

The only problem was my secret: I had bridge cables for ham-
strings, which severely limited my range of motion. I was easily
the stiffest yogi in most of the classes I attended, so how was I
going to teach anyone yoga when I couldn't even touch my own
toes? I decided to overlook my perceived shortcoming and just
take the next step. Maybe I would cultivate flexibility (I hoped).

I enrolled in a 200-hour yoga teacher training at my local yoga studio. Whenever it came time for me to demonstrate a pose while surrounded by my fellow yoga teachers in training, I grew nervous, insecure, and sweaty. I prayed that either the moment would pass quickly, or that my body would somehow defy the laws of physiology and my range of motion would spontaneously increase. Of course, neither happened. But to my surprise, no one ever mentioned my stiffness during the training.

Upon graduation, what I lacked in flexibility I made up for in hustle. I was willing to drive all over town to teach anyone, anywhere, at any time, paid or for free. But whenever I taught, I rarely demonstrated poses out of the fear that I would be exposed as a fraud.

Coincidentally, I had to quickly become an expert at giving verbal cues to yogis of various experience levels while properly managing the clock and tending to my music playlist (any one of those skills can take a yoga teacher many years to master). At the same time, I made sure to always offer words of encouragement, like, "Yoga is not about the poses. Rather, it's about connecting to a deeper, more authentic place within, a place of acceptance," blah blah blah.

Did I really believe that, or did I feel more like a dentist with two missing front teeth who was afraid to smile? It depended on the day. But despite my neuroses, my class sizes grew from just a few people to around ten. The next year I was averaging fifteen people per class. Then twenty. Either people knew my secret and didn't care, or I'd turned into the David Copperfield of yoga teachers and had mastered the art of smoke and mirrors.

I slowly began to realize from talking to my students how my carefully guarded secret was a far bigger deal to me than it was to anyone else. What they appreciated was my ability to relate to yogis of all levels, and especially to beginners.

My gift was in making everyone feel good right where they were. Newbies felt safe in my classes because I encouraged them to take it slow, and I *always* made a point to love on the stiff people. My more experienced students appreciated how I spoke about the practice as a metaphor for meeting challenges in life, with more acceptance of where we are and less judgment for where we are restricted.

Others reported that I was far less egotistical and more compassionate than many of my more bendy colleagues. And a few came just for the great music playlists that I would spend hours preparing before each class—because if you're going to play music, it may as well be amazing.

As it turned out, not being flexible was more of an asset than a liability.

"It's not about wishing you had something you don't," I would preach, "but asking yourself, 'How can I do the most with what I have right now?'" This became one of the mantras

I repeated often in class—words I so desperately needed to hear myself again and again.

The pivotal moment, when I was finally able to let go of the self-judgment that had haunted me since my very first yoga class, came about four years after I started teaching. It was during a sunset hike with my buddy Will, who was one of my yoga mentors.

He knew of my secret, and although we'd never had a conversation about it up to that point, he asked me half-jokingly, "So how does it feel to be one of the most popular yoga teachers in Los Angeles who can't even touch his own toes?" I remember my heart tightening and suddenly being at a loss for words.

He sensed my apprehension, and after a moment of awkward silence where I was fishing for the perfect "spiritual" reply, he answered his own question: "You know, a wise man once told me, you don't have to beat Michael Jordan in a game of basketball in order to coach him to a championship."

And that was the moment I found comfort in the discomfort of being the stiffest yoga teacher in Los Angeles.

This begs the question: what if *your* greatest secret was also your biggest asset? The Spiritual Minimalist is willing to sit in the discomfort of the unknown in order to take the leap of faith in the direction of their purpose. That means you must be willing to follow your curiosity even though you have no idea how it's going to turn out, which is more often the case than not. And if you're committed to making a lifestyle out of following your heart, you *have* to make friends with discomfort. To the Spiritual Minimalist, that discomfort is a telltale sign that you are indeed moving in the direction of your potential.

YOUR HEART IS WATCHING

You ever announce a big plan, commitment, or goal and expect everyone to excitedly rally around you, but all you hear are crickets? It's very tempting in those quiet moments to start questioning your goal or reconsidering your plan, or to back out of your commitment.

Well, here's the secret: we're testing you—meaning, *the world* is testing you. Society wants to see how serious you are, whether you're just floating an idea out there for "likes" or approval and applause, or whether you're doing it because you are committed to your vision and something deep inside of you is inspiring you to go the long haul.

We want to see that you're not going to let our lukewarm response deter you, that you're not going to allow a little rejection to slow you down, and that you're not going to let a lack of accountability or support stop you. We want to see that you're going to do it anyway, even though it seems like no one is watching and no one cares.

And if you do it anyway, even if at times you feel like you're all on your own, your insatiable passion will eventually attract a helper. And then another, and another.

And that's how ninety-nine percent of movements are formed, with one person who is so passionate about change that they are unwilling to let the discomfort of putting themselves out there stop them from taking the leap.

The Spiritual Minimalist becomes proficient in taking leaps of faith. They never consider giving up on their inner calling, no matter how uncomfortable the idea of failure makes them feel. Instead, when the time is right, they give in to the discomfort and allow their heart to guide them to the next step along their path.

The world may not be watching you right now, but your heart is always watching—and that's what the world desperately needs more of: individuals who are unafraid to stay loyal to their heart.

ACTION: THE RESTING SQUAT

Speaking of finding comfort in discomfort, Spiritual Minimalists take that instruction quite literally and train themselves to sit in discomfort by mastering the resting squat.

Have you ever tried to sit in a resting squat? Although we are born with the hip flexibility to sit in a squat, with time, age, and our sedentary Western lifestyle, we gradually lose that ability. Too much sitting in chairs, in cars, and at desks weakens the mobility in our hips, and as a result we develop tight hips, which puts more strain on our ankles, knees, and back—and that can lead to major health problems downstream.

But now that you're actively practicing Spiritual Minimalism, it's time to restore balance in the Universe by regaining your natural hip flexibility. Because as it turns out, the resting squat is one of the most beneficial stretches that you can and should do on a daily basis, especially with all of the flaneur-ing you've been doing while following your curiosity (see page 128 to read more about flaneur-ing).

Sitting in a squat will help you improve your posture, flexibility, mobility, and metabolism and burn calories. Your lower body and core will become stronger and you will be less susceptible to injuries and disease. If you are experiencing any knee pain or back pain, or if you just want to be more flexible but you haven't made the time for yoga, a five-minute resting squat is the one stretch that every Spiritual Minimalist with the appropriate range of motion should start working into their morning routine.

How to sit in a resting squat:

Stand straight up and place your feet at shoulder width apart (or a little wider if your hips are exceptionally tight). Then bend your knees and squat down until your legs are completely bent while at the same time keeping your back as straight as possible.

If you can't bend your knees that deeply without your heels coming off the floor, then you can sit on a block or a low table, or you can place a book or a towel under each of your heels for leverage. The important thing is that you get your hips below your knees.

Then place both arms on the insides of your legs and bring your hands together in the prayer position, and pray for mercy for neglecting your hips all these years. Seriously, try to sit in the squat for up to thirty seconds to start. And then using your hands, gradually lean back and gently lower yourself onto the floor. Lean over to one side and carefully stand back up.

Eventually, you want to be able to stand back up directly from the squat without using your hands. But to start, feel free to sit on the floor and stay there until you get the circulation going in your legs before standing back up. Otherwise, you could make yourself a little dizzy by standing up too quickly.

Sitting in a resting squat can be intense, hence the opportunity to find comfort in discomfort. But since you're probably new to this level of discomfort, here's a suggestion to make the time go by faster. Once you slowly build up to five minutes in the squat (after several weeks or months of daily practice), I suggest listening to a five-minute song or watching a five-minute educational video on YouTube, or setting an alarm and catching up on your social media while you're squatting.

Eventually, you can treat this as more of a meditation and squat without any other stimulation (if that's your preference). But the important thing is that you're making the time to increase flexibility in your joints. And whatever distraction or stimulation you need to assist your goal of working up to five minutes will be a small price to pay for long-term mobility and good health.

CELEBRATION

If you have to take the stairs today, the Spiritual Minimalist treats it as a celebration of their legs. If you have to lift something heavy, treat it as a celebration of your strength. If you have to do something alone, treat it as a celebration of your independence. If you have to be around someone who's annoying, treat it as a celebration of your patience. And if you find yourself in a lemon of a situation, look for ways to turn it into lemonade.

SCARY YES

Some motivational speakers say that if an idea or a proposition doesn't elicit a "hell yes," then don't even bother—which is cute, but the Spiritual Minimalist sees acting on a "hell yes" as easy and obvious. If something is a "hell yes," of course you're going to do it.

But what the Spiritual Minimalist finds particularly intriguing is a "scary yes."

Want to take an ice bath during the winter?

What about starting that podcast you've been telling yourself you wanted to start for the last three years?

Or going to therapy to figure out why you keep dating narcissists?

Or how about attending that addiction recovery program (finally)?

Those kinds of yeses are scary because they force you out of your comfort zone and into your growth zone. But once you act on a scary yes, you discover a few very interesting things: 1) it's no longer as scary, 2) you're more apt to do other things that are scary, and 3) if something's not at least initially scary, you're not likely to grow from it. So start saying "yes" to more of the things that scare you—not because they are dangerous, but because they help you access your potential.

COUNTING YOUR REPS

How to ensure you optimize your mental and physical health for life? Simple: move. Daily movement is a requirement for any serious Spiritual Minimalist. And don't wait until you feel like it to exercise, because most of the time, you won't feel like it, or you'll tell yourself you don't have the time, or you won't know how to move.

We're going to cover how to exercise like a Spiritual Minimalist later in this section. But there's one element of exercise that a Spiritual Minimalist can use to make the experience more inspired, and that is how you count your repetitions, or "reps."

Instead of mindlessly counting the number of reps you do with boring old numbers, you're going to practice counting with affirmations. In other words, if you're doing a set of five push-ups, you usually count each push-up sequentially: 1—2—3—4—5.

There's of course nothing wrong with this, but what if you could count your push-ups while also counting your blessings? This means, even when exercising, you can do less and accomplish more! All you're going to do is replace the numbers with the words of your chosen affirmation.

For instance, with those same five push-ups, instead of counting from 1 to 5, choose a five-word affirmation, and treat each word of the affirmation as a rep count:

1. I
2. am
3. worthy
4. of
5. love

So instead of counting 1–2–3–4–5, you'll count by saying, either out loud or to yourself, "I–am–worthy–of–love." And you'll keep repeating that affirmation each time you do a five-rep exercise. As you practice your affirmations, you know what will happen? You will be getting physically *and* emotionally stronger, because you will feel more worthy of love by the end of your set.

Now, when first starting out, it's going to feel silly, because it's not normally how people count reps. But normal is synonymous with ungrateful. So you have to ask yourself, do you want to be normal and ungrateful, or do you want to be uncommon and grateful? Because as a Spiritual Minimalist, you're going to be doing a lot of things that are not normal. There's no love in being normal. There's no mindfulness in it. There's no gratitude. And that begs the question, why aim for normalcy at all, in any area of life?

But if you bring the mindfulness and the gratitude into your most basic of tasks, chores, routines, and habits, you will optimize each moment of your day. A simple experience of sweeping up will become a highlight of your day. Doing a set of push-ups can be transformative.

As a Spiritual Minimalist, you're training yourself to approach *everything* in life from the inside-out, as opposed to what most normal people are doing, which is viewing the quality of their life from the outside-in.

On the opposite page, you'll find some affirmations that you can practice with for various rep counts. If you don't connect with these affirmations, take some time to make up your own to correspond with whatever your average rep count is, and write them on a sheet of paper that you'll keep next to you for reference when you exercise. With practice, you will commit them to memory and, for you, exercise will double as a powerful spiritual experience, not just boring old movements.

WHAT'S IN MY BAG: A RESISTANCE BAND

A Spiritual Minimalist is consistently on the move—and I don't mean always traveling. I mean, always understanding the importance of daily movement known as resistance training. Most people facilitate their daily resistance training by going to a local gym. But not the Spiritual Minimalist. The Spiritual

1. I
2. am
3. blessed

1. I
2. am
3. loved

1. Gratitude
2. is
3. my
4. super
5. power

1. I
2. am
3. creating
4. my
5. future

1. I
2. deserve
3. to
4. be
5. happy

1. I
2. am
3. worthy
4. of
5. love

1. I
2. am
3. in
4. the
5. right
6. place
7. at
8. the
9. right
10. time

1. My
2. life
3. is
4. blessed
5. and
6. I
7. love
8. who
9. I
10. am

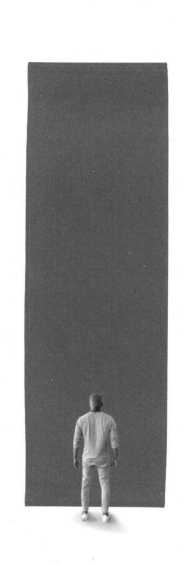

Minimalist brings the gym to her, wherever she happens to be, with the help of a simple but effective resistance band.

A resistance band turns an otherwise ordinary, unremarkable hotel room or Airbnb into a mini gym as you can execute a number of resistance exercises that help to build strength in each major body part while only occupying minimal space and weight in your bag. It has multiuse functionality for completing a thorough minimalist workout. To that end, here are five exercises to try over the next five days using your trusty resistance band.

Leg day: the banded squat

Stand with your feet slightly wider than shoulder width apart, and with your toes angled out slightly. Step on the inside of your band with both feet and loop the rest of the band around your shoulders. While sticking your chest out and keeping your back as straight as possible, begin to bend your knees like you're going to sit in an imaginary chair placed behind you. Stop at the point before you start straining, and then, grounding into all four corners of both feet, press back up to the standing position. As you go through this motion, make sure that your knees don't buckle in and that your back doesn't round. If either happens, you may need a lighter band, or perhaps practice air squats with no band first to get the movement down. Start with 25 to 50 reps in sets of 5.

Count with affirmations instead of numbers (see "Counting Your Reps" on page 149).

Shoulder day: seated shoulder press

Step into your band like you're putting on pants, hook the band around your butt, and then sit down on the band with your legs crossed. The top of the band should be resting loosely on your thighs. Next, spread the loose part of the band as wide as your knees, and grab ahold of the band near each knee. Keeping your hands knee-distance apart, rotate your arms so your knuckles are facing up, bringing the top of the band just under your chin. (The band will be pressed against the outsides of your forearms.) Then, start to straighten your back and press your arms up toward the sky, sticking your chest out in the process. After a brief pause at the top of the movement, bend your elbows until the band is just below your chin again. You should feel this movement in your shoulders, not in your back. If there's any pain, stop and do pike push-ups instead. (You can search variations of both exercises on YouTube.) Otherwise, continue to the next rep by pressing your arms straight up again, then lowering them back down. See if you can do 25 to 50 reps in sets of 5.

Back day: bent-over rows or assisted pull-ups

Sit with your legs straight out in front of you and, with your resistance band folded into a line, wrap your band around your feet. The loops of the band should now be sticking out on either side of your legs. Reach down and grab ahold of a loop in each fist, and turn your fists so your palms face down. Or, if you want more of a challenge, slide your hands down the band toward your feet. Next, while sitting up as straight as possible and engaging your core, stick your chest out and slowly bend your elbows back, pulling the band as if you are rowing. As you do this, your shoulder blades should squeeze together. Then return to the start position by straightening your arms in the direction of your feet, and repeat. Keep your chest out, shoulders back, and core engaged the entire time. See if you can do 25 to 50 reps in sets of 5.

Alternatively, you can use your band to do assisted pull-ups. If you have access to a pull-up bar, wrap your band around the bar and pull the loop through itself. Stick one foot or your knee into the open end of the band that's hanging down. And after you feel securely anchored in the band, grab the bar with both hands, and pull yourself up. See if you can do 25 to 50 reps in sets of 5.

Chest day: banded push-ups

If you can't do a regular, full-extension push-up, then you don't need a band for this. Try doing 25 or 50 push-ups in sets of 5 without the band. If you need to drop your knees to the floor in order to keep good form in your upper body, then make that adjustment. As you build more strength in your arms and chest, you'll be able to do unmodified push-ups in no time. When doing an unmodified push-up becomes relatively easy for you, then try the banded push-ups by holding one side of the band in each hand with the band wrapped around the back of your shoulders. Next, get in the push-up position and see if you can do 25 to 50 normal-paced (not fast), full-extension push-ups with good form in sets of 5. It'll be harder than you think as the band resists your effort each time you push up.

Arm day: banded bicep curls and triceps pulls

Last but not least in our full-body Spiritual Minimalist workout, we can't leave out the arms. To get or maintain strong biceps and triceps, I recommend doing some banded bicep curls followed by triceps pulls. All you need is your band and a door.

Bicep Curls: With the door ajar, hook the band about 6 inches (10 cm) under the bottom of the door. Standing about a foot directly in front of the open door (so that you can see both knobs), grab the band with each hand

and position your hands far enough down the band to feel a challenging amount of tension. With your feet solidly grounded, your back straight, and your knees slightly bent, start bending your arms, curling the band toward your chest. Then reset by straightening your arms, and repeat for another rep.

Try not to sway your upper body back and forth with the reps. Hold steady and let your biceps (the front of your upper arms) do *all* of the work. The only part of your body moving should be your forearms moving up toward your chest and back to the starting position. If this feels too challenging, loosen your grip on the band until you find the right amount of tension to do 5 reps without swaying. And if you don't have a door, you can step on the band with one foot and curl from there. Try for 25 to 50 reps in sets of 5.

Triceps Pulls: When you're done polishing up your guns, unhook the band from the bottom of the door and hook it onto the top of the door. Your stance is going to be the same as it was for the bicep curls, except this time you're going to grab the band with your elbows bent. Then, with a slight upper body tilt toward the door, you're going to straighten your arms in the direction of your feet, flexing your triceps (the backs of your upper arms) in the process. After fully extending both arms, reset by bending your elbows back to the start position, and repeat for another rep. Try a total of 25 to 50 reps in sets of 5.

To get and stay in optimum shape, repeat this full-body workout each week, increasing the number of reps until you can do 100 of each exercise. As you get stronger, feel free to explore different variations and play with the rep counts and rest times for each set. Incorporate the rep-counting method we discussed earlier in this section. YouTube is also full of videos showing every variation under the sun.

I dedicate the same day each week to a specific body part, so I don't have to think about it. I know that Mondays are always chest days, and Tuesdays are leg days. Wednesdays are back days. Thursdays, I do an asymmetrical leg exercise, such as walking lunges. And Fridays are arm days. No matter where I am or how busy I get, I always carve out ten to fifteen minutes to do my daily movement. And as a Spiritual Minimalist, you should too.

PRINCIPLE 7:

The Freedom of Choicelessness

"When you do everything in your power to make it work and it's still not working, the Universe is trying to save your ass."

—The Spiritual Minimalist

FINDING YOUR PURPOSE

After work on Thursday, December 1, forty-two-year old Rosa Parks boarded the Cleveland Avenue bus at around 6 pm in downtown Montgomery, Alabama. The year was 1955, and during that time, Black people were banned from riding in the front rows of city buses. Mrs. Parks paid her fare and sat in the first row of the section designated for "colored" riders.

As the bus bumped and burped its way down the avenue, the "whites only" section began to quickly fill up, and the bus driver noticed that two or three white men were standing. So at the next stop, the driver demanded that all four Black passengers who were sitting in the first row of the colored section give up their seats so the white passengers could sit down. Three of the Black riders complied. But Mrs. Parks chose not to. She later said that she felt a determination cover her body like a warm quilt on a winter night.

"Why don't you stand up?" the driver barked. When she told him that she shouldn't have to give up her seat, he got the police to arrest Mrs. Parks.

Rosa Parks had no way of knowing that her act of defiance in that moment would initiate one of the largest and most successful mass movements in U.S. history: a 381-day city-wide bus boycott, which would launch an unknown twenty-six-year-old reverend named Martin Luther King, Jr. to international acclaim, resulting in a march on Washington where King would deliver one of the most iconic speeches of the twentieth century, the passage of a voting rights act, a Nobel Peace Prize, a national holiday, and so much more.

"People always say that I didn't give up my seat because I was tired," recalled Mrs. Parks. "But that isn't true. I was no more tired than I usually was at the end of a working day. No, the only tired I was, was tired of giving in."

We sometimes mistake our job for our purpose. But Rosa Parks worked as a seamstress. She wasn't an entrepreneur or a celebrity. Yet it was her act of defiance on that fateful day that initiated the modern civil rights movement. And that became the purpose that she didn't even know she had until after she found herself in that situation—coming home from a long day of work, sitting in her bus seat, and feeling tired of giving in.

Many people these days spend a lot of time contemplating their purpose, wondering if and when they will find it—as if it's some sort of cosmic Easter egg hunt. But a Spiritual Minimalist takes a different approach to purpose. As a Spiritual Minimalist, you want to first get crystal clear about your core principles and values. Then, all you have to do is start living by them to the best of your ability. And as long as you're loyal to your values while following your curiosity, you can also assume that, like Rosa Parks, you're going to end up right where you're supposed to be.

In other words, if a decision feels aligned with your values, then no matter how scary it is or how inconvenient it becomes, you act. But if it *doesn't* feel aligned with your values, then no matter how glittery it is or how profitable it can be, you pass. While living by your core values may feel restrictive at first, it's actually quite liberating. Because you no longer have to wonder if you will do the right thing. You've already pre-determined that you will do the right thing, as dictated by your values. And your resolve to honor your values provides you a sense of freedom: the freedom of choicelessness.

No matter what happens, your values have already decided your course of action. For instance, one of your values can be to always honor your word. At first that seems restrictive. But if you live by that value, you will be very careful what you say you will do, which gives your word more power. Because once you say it, it's done. There's no further need to deliberate. Another value may be to stand up to injustice. This doesn't mean you have to take on every injustice on the planet. But like Mrs. Parks, when you've had one of those days where you're tired of giving in, and your heart voice is urging you to take a stand, you take a stand. Make yourself choiceless in that moment. If you remain loyal to your principles and values in that way, you can assume that you are also living your purpose.

Exercise

In order to live by your core principles and values, you have to know what they are. So here's a quick thought experiment that will help you identify them: imagine that you are witnessing your own memorial service. Your family and friends are going up to the podium to offer reflections about your life. What would you want them to say about you? Would you want them to remark about how generous you were? How you found the humor in everyday situations? How you would often go out of your way to help those in need? How you always honored your word?

After spending some time thinking about what you would want those who knew you to say about you at the end of your life, see what themes emerge. Those themes represent your core values and principles. Write out as many as you'd like, and then consolidate where appropriate. By the end, you may have a list of three to five core values, such as:

Always go the extra mile

See the best in others

Trust my intuition

Stand up to injustice

Don't take myself too seriously

Again, living by your values shouldn't be viewed as a prison sentence, because these are *your* values, assigned by you, based on how you ultimately want to be remembered. On the contrary, there's immense freedom in knowing what you stand for and are willing to fight for. Being clear about your values will allow you to focus your attention and energy on what's truly important while not wasting energy on things that don't feel aligned with what you're here to do.

YOUR FINAL IMPRESSION

When a business or love relationship ends, how do you exit? With grace? With thoughtful consideration? By honoring your commitments?

We put a lot of importance on making good first impressions, but we sometimes underestimate the lasting impact of our final impression.

Anyone doing anything of note will over time develop a reputation, which can either inspire or repel people who haven't yet met you in person.

Most "bad" reputations are the result of repeated failures to leave a positive last impression. For instance, can anyone say the following about you?

"She quit without giving two-weeks' notice."

"He broke up with me via text message."

"He never said thanks after I went out of my way to help him."

"She never showed up to our meeting and didn't call."

Some of these impressions for which you can be remembered forever are ridiculously small oversights that can still easily be

corrected by saying thank you, giving someone a heads up, apologizing, or just by listening.

Your first impression is the one that sets the tone, but your last impression is the one that cements your reputation. How you leave a friendship, partnership, or relationship is far more important than how it started. And as a Spiritual Minimalist, every day you are presented with another opportunity to upgrade your past impressions and design your reputation in a way that best reflects how you ultimately want to be remembered.

Whatever the exit story is, remember that it will be told over and over and embellished with time. The effects of this can be amazing if you exited with grace or unnecessarily embarrassing if it was messy.

Instead of having to spend years giving context to the "grapevine" version of the story, just do now what you should've done back then to clean up the mess—apologize, forgive, acknowledge the other person's experience, be honest about yours, etc. Sure, cleaning up the mess may be hard for your ego and time-consuming, but it allows you the freedom to do more of what you're here to do while cementing a reputation that inspires support along the way.

A BOOKMARK MOMENT

When I interview people on my podcast, I look for ordinary people who've found their purpose by turning their life around in some extraordinary way—which usually means they reached a point in their life when they started living by their values.

More often than not, there was a day when, like Rosa Parks in the story that opens this chapter, they found themselves backed into a corner. And they probably could've lied to themselves about it, or they could've pretended like it wasn't happening. Instead, they said, "Enough is enough. I'm going to do something different than what I've been doing. I'm going to start telling a different story about my life. I'm finally going to face my truth."

And they stood up to injustice, or they made amends, or they started what ultimately grew into a movement, or they committed to a larger mission, or they took quitting off the table. Whatever it was, that day became a bookmark moment in their life.

And when they are known widely enough to write books, deliver speeches, and give podcast interviews about their story, they recount their "Rosa Parks moment" over and over and over. That's all anybody wants to hear about—what happened on that day when they decided enough is enough? What were they feeling? What obstacles were they facing? How did they find the courage to say enough is enough?

And here's the key takeaway: as you're getting closer to your pain threshold, where you're tired of giving in, that day for you can be today. As a Spiritual Minimalist, you have an opportunity to do something today that can change the direction of the rest of your life. Today, you can establish a boundary around what you are no longer willing to tolerate.

And if you're courageous enough to stick to it, five and ten and twenty years from now, you'll be telling stories about what happened today—stories that will continue to make others say "wow" and inspire those who hear about what you did (and even those who haven't yet been born) to feel the courage you showed today is possible for them to have as well.

Or, today can just be another day that blends in with all of the rest of the forgettable days where you didn't stand up, where you didn't take the leap, where you continued to allow the status quo to dictate how your life plays out.

Either way, it's up to you to seize the day. And when you eventually do, in time, you will solidify your Spiritual Minimalist status, and I would be honored to have you come onto my podcast to share the story of what happened next. I'm already looking forward to marveling at your courage during our interview.

ACTION: HAND-WASH YOUR CLOTHES

When I first went nomadic, I got a twenty-two-inch carry-on bag because it was the biggest bag that they allow you to stow in the overhead bins of airplanes. I thought I was being clever, but what I realized later was that I wasn't asking the right question. Instead of asking how much I could fit into a twenty-two-inch carry-on bag, the better question is, *what is the smallest number of items I truly need?* And here's the thing: you won't know the answer to that question unless you intentionally practice restricting yourself.

If you try to restrict yourself to a suitcase, you will fill up the suitcase and swear that you need everything in it. If you only have a carry-on bag, you will fill that up. If you only have a backpack, you will fill it up. And if you only have a daypack, you will fill it up and swear that you need everything in it to live. The truth is, you need much less than you think. One of the discoveries I made about a year into my journey was how to create more space by hand-washing my clothes. Once I started doing that, I was able to dramatically cut down the size of my capsule wardrobe while lightening my load, without sacrificing variety.

Hand-washing gave me much more freedom because I could do more with fewer clothes. Traveling light is less about restriction and more about becoming adaptable to any environment. Remember, the less adaptable you are, the less present you are.

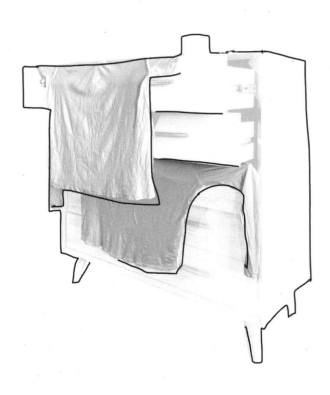

You may be able to fool everybody into thinking that you're present, but your body will know the truth. If your luggage gets lost and you are low-key worried that you don't have whatever you think you need for your trip, you won't be as present as you would be if, deep down, you knew that lost or ruined luggage could not affect your internal state.

You may not have to hand-wash your clothes often, but when you do, it will make all of the difference in allowing you to be relaxed and present versus anxious and worried, which is far from the most attractive version of you. And it's best to practice and perfect your hand-washing skills when you don't need to hand-wash—meaning, right now while you're at home.

Here's what you'll need to hand-wash your clothes on the road:

Shampoo

Why not bar soap or body wash? Because it doesn't lather as well on your clothes. But if body wash or bar soap is all you have, then use that.

A water source

You can use a sink, a tub, or you can even wash your clothes while taking a shower if you're pressed for time.

A towel

You need a dry hand towel for wringing out smaller clothing items post-wash, or a large body towel for wringing out bigger items like jeans, chinos, and sweatshirts.

The process:

1. Soak your clothes while filling the sink with water.
2. Turn off the water and apply a dab of shampoo to the clothes.
3. Rub the fabric together for a couple of minutes, or until the soap fully lathers on the clothing.
4. For tough stains, rub and agitate for twice as long.
5. Drain the water and thoroughly rinse the shampoo or soap out of the clothing.
6. Wring out the article of clothing as best as you can.
7. Roll the article of clothing into your hand towel and wring it out again with the towel by twisting it 8 to 10 times. DO NOT skip this step or your clothes will take much longer to dry.
8. Unroll the towel and hang the article of clothing on a hanger, or on the back of a chair, or on a hook in the room.
9. If it's not too humid, the clothing will be completely dry and ready to wear again within about five hours.

10. I like to hand-wash my clothes at night before bed, and they are usually dry by morning.

Don't wait until you're on the road to practice. Give it a try today. Start by hand-washing one article of clothing at a time, something small like a T-shirt or underwear. You'll work out the kinks with a little practice. Once you get the hang of it, the entire process should take no more than about five to ten minutes.

If you want to go further, for one week, restrict yourself to only wearing clothes that you hand-wash. That will give you the freedom of choicelessness and force you to practice. Depending on your lifestyle, you don't need to wash your pants or sweaters as often, but you should practice hand-washing larger items of clothing as well, just in case. And you can always refer to YouTube for specifics about how to hand-wash more delicate items.

HARDLY PAYING ATTENTION

As a senior in high school, I was spending so much time figuring out what to wear each day that I eventually began to question whether anyone was even paying attention to my outfits.

So, as an experiment, I decided to wear the same purple top and khaki pants every day for a week, just to see if anyone would notice or say anything about it. By the end of the week, no one had said a word.

I concluded that the majority of people aren't paying attention to what we're doing or not doing—mostly because they're so preoccupied with whatever *they're* doing or not doing.

It's been a liberating reminder throughout my life, particularly when it comes to taking important personal and professional risks. And I'm sure the same is true for you.

As a practicing Spiritual Minimalist, if you're hesitant to take a chance because you're afraid of what others may think, remember this: *they're hardly paying attention.* So go for it!

WHAT'S IN MY BAG: MY CAPSULE WARDROBE

As a Spiritual Minimalist, one of the best ways to embody the freedom of choicelessness is by assembling a capsule wardrobe, which can serve as your daily uniform to save time and effort in picking out clothes to wear each day. If you're up for the challenge, before getting rid of half the clothes in your closet, start experimenting with what you actually wear on a regular basis. Imagine that you have to travel this weekend and you can only bring two outfits; which ones would you bring? After you narrow the options down to a

handful of looks, see if you can wear only those articles of clothing over the next week.

Here's what I currently have in my capsule wardrobe rotation:

One pair of dark chinos

You want this to be your best-fitting pair of pants, and you want them to be dark, because you may sit on something dirty, or you may accidentally spill something in your lap while eating or drinking, and you don't want to look like a slob. Plus, this will ideally be the only pair of pants in your capsule wardrobe, so choose well.

One lightweight cotton button-down shirt or dressy top

This will serve as your formal wear, for a special occasion. It should be a well-fitting white or dark top, preferably not colored. I like white, because in the worst-case scenario, if it gets stained, it's easier to make it white again with a good hand-wash and maybe a little bleach. If you don't have an iron, you can just lay it flat after hand-washing.

A neutral-colored zip-up hoodie

Your hoodie will come in handy when the weather is a bit cooler than anticipated, and the hoodie can serve as protection in case it drizzles. If you have a blazer, you can wear the hoodie under the blazer for an extra layer of warmth if needed. Or, you can wear it to your workout if you're outside and it's a little cool.

A white short-sleeve cotton T-shirt and a long-sleeve shirt

I definitely recommend getting white or dark shirts because they are easier to keep clean, especially if you accidentally spill greasy food on your clothes.

A dark cashmere sweater or lightweight cardigan

For cooler weather, your sweater can go over your dress shirt or top for a classier look, or be tied around your waist as a backup in case you have a cooler-than-usual night.

A pair of elastic workout shorts or tights

When it's time for your daily exercise, these will be your workout shorts. Men, if your shorts fit you well, they can also double as your swim trunks in case you find yourself around a swimmable body of water.

A lightweight blazer or jacket

In case you have to conduct business, this is a classy article of clothing to go over your dress shirt, sweater, or hoodie, depending on the occasion.

Meditation shawl

I talk more about the meditation shawl in another section (see "What's in My Bag: My Meditation Shawl" on page 41). You can wrap it around your neck to keep warm in colder climates.

White shoes

There's another section about the white shoe recommendation (see "What's in My Bag: The White Shoe" on page 134). Basically, any shoe that you can dress up or down and easily keep clean should go into your capsule wardrobe.

Obviously, you don't need to get the same articles of clothing as I have. Women may want to include a dress, a skirt, some jeans. The overall point is to wear clothing that pairs well with your other clothes, and only keep articles of clothing that you love and wear often—not items that you kind of like, sometimes, in the right light, and at the right angle. Instead, wear clothes that fit you amazingly, that you are regularly complimented in. That's the Spiritual Minimalist standard.

If you don't absolutely love it, don't buy it. And if you find something else that you think you love, but you don't love it enough to replace one of your current articles of clothing with it, then it doesn't meet the standard. If you truly loved it, you would be okay with swapping it with something you already own that you love less. That's how you exercise the freedom of choicelessness with your Spiritual Minimalist capsule wardrobe.

Conclusion

"Reading self-help books does not qualify
as 'inner work.' Inner work happens when you
put what you read and learn into practice."

—The Spiritual Minimalist

TIME TO INTEGRATE

Now that we've covered all seven principles, ideally you will take your time to embody those principles that resonate with you the most and have fun incorporating the corresponding actions into your daily life.

The only principle that I would strongly suggest making a non-negotiable is your daily meditation practice. Meditation is the key habit that can make embodying all of the other principles much easier. It will allow you to do less while accomplishing more in every area of life. For instance, if you wanted to begin with embracing choicelessness but you haven't yet begun cultivating inner happiness, then it will be much harder to see choicelessness as freedom, as opposed to a limitation. Prioritize your meditation, and all of the other principles will be easier to integrate.

I also recommend that you continue revisiting the concepts and stories in this book. Just pick it up whenever the mood strikes and flip through it to see what catches your eye. As you embody these seven principles, the stories and practices related to each principle will take on new meaning and significance with time.

If you experienced the book in a more random fashion, consider going back and reading it linearly, from cover to cover. You will most definitely discover passages that you missed or sections that didn't resonate as much the first time. Likewise, if you've already read *Travel Light* from cover to cover, try perusing it randomly and see what you discover.

In the meantime, prepare to hear your heart voice more clearly. But hearing it is one thing. See what happens when you become intentional about acting upon it—especially in those in-between moments, when you're in traffic or while you're standing in line at the pharmacy.

Whenever you are feeling like you are lacking something, practice giving that very thing. And follow your curiosity as often as you can, even if it makes you uncomfortable to do so.

That's an opportunity to find comfort in discomfort. And whenever you're at a crossroads, make a decision based on your values. This is the Spiritual Minimalist way—the way to travel *light*.

Here is a summary of the daily Spiritual Minimalist practices recommended in this book:

- Meditate fifteen to twenty minutes each morning
- Practice following your heart voice as often as you can
- Play the gratitude game during your in-between moments
- Leave spaces better than you found them
- Make a habit of walking more and flaneur-ing
- Sit in a resting squat each morning
- Practice hand-washing your clothes

As I've witnessed in my own experience (and as a meditation teacher for over fifteen years), reaching mastery of any new habit or practice is far from a linear process. Here's what I have learned about the process and what you will likely experience.

Mastery is a process of learning something new, applying it in a controlled environment, failing, asking questions, reapplying with new understanding, refining your approach, realizing that you're not actually failing even when it feels like you are, redefining success, breaking down old indoctrinations, doing homework, relearning how to learn, replacing your old habits, "failing" again, asking better questions, going back and doing it the wrong way just to see how far you've come, "failing" yet again, doing more homework, getting lucky, "failing," then casting doubt on the whole thing.

After stopping for a while, you will experience an unexpected crisis, then return to the path with humility, re-experiencing it as if for the first time, getting reinspired, following the protocol with more confidence, asking more nuanced questions, making your new habits nonnegotiable, becoming process-oriented as opposed to outcome-oriented, redefining success yet again, taking tiny steps just to keep forward momentum, setting smaller goals, reviewing your past trajectory, adjusting for common mistakes, preempting future "failures" before they happen, adapting to change more easily, completely letting go of the outcome, and committing to something larger than yourself.

I could keep going, but you get the point: mastery is multi-layered, multifaceted, and dynamic, and therefore it is sometimes confusing to know where you are in the process. But that's precisely what it means to be "in the process." And the more you stop thinking of mastery in linear terms, the faster you will advance. So enjoy your Spiritual Minimalist experiments, and know that you can't mess up. Any experience is useful for achieving mastery.

You also never have to refer to this as "Spiritual Minimalism." This is just a different way to approach life, and if you find that you get a lot of value from it, then keep doing it. And if, after trying it out, you feel that it doesn't add the type of value that you're interested in, then just keep it as a point of reference for what's possible, and maybe return to it later. Either way, these principles are yours to do with as you wish. My only hope for you is that you continue exploring all that life has to offer, and that you allow yourself to be driven more by your curiosity than by your fears.

KEEP PRACTICING

I'd like to leave you with one last story about something I experienced back before I started intentionally traveling light.

I was walking by myself through an outdoor promenade in Santa Monica, California, late one night after an evening of salsa dancing. On the way to my car, I heard someone singing "La Bamba" off in the distance. So naturally I followed my curiosity to see who would be outdoors at midnight in an empty promenade performing "La Bamba."

As I got closer, I saw a young man, probably thirteen or fourteen, dancing and gyrating with such enthusiasm and passion while covering Ritchie Valens's popular song.

His worn-out mic and speaker kept cutting off and on. But he continued stomping and spinning around as though he was performing onstage at Madison Square Garden in front of tens of thousands. He sang more covers, and I was absolutely mesmerized.

Soon after, another guy stopped to watch. And then a woman. We were three of maybe five people in the entire promenade at that time of night. And throughout his performance, we kept glancing over at one another with amazement. I remember wishing more people had been there to see it.

I took down the singer's information and looked him up when I got home, and I wasn't surprised to see that he was all over the internet. He'd been performing since he was seven. He'd been on *The Ellen Show*. He had even performed in front of President Obama. How fortunate was I to have a private show in the middle of the night in Santa Monica, while his mother sat patiently in her car a block away, waiting for him to finish. His dedication to his craft was palpable.

A few years later, I was strolling through an outdoor promenade in Boulder, Colorado, and there he was again, still performing, gyrating, and singing with that same degree of energy and fervor—the result of perhaps thousands upon thousands of hours of practice. Clearly this was his gift, and you felt it deep inside if you ever watched him perform. He was someone who was truly living his purpose.

One night, he posted an update to his social media feed that has lingered with me ever since I read it. It was just one line: "Keep practicing, even if it seems like it's hopeless."

And I will offer to you the same sentiment. Even after successfully hearing and following your heart voice, you can reach moments of uncertainty. Even after following your curiosity, you may still feel lost and devoid of purpose. Even when you give what you want to receive and make decisions based on your values, you can feel like you're not where you should be. That is all a part of the process. And while the thought of showing up over and over and making frequent mistakes can seem tedious, it is the quickest way to embody the seven principles of Spiritual Minimalism. So don't strive for perfection. Instead, aim for consistency. And no matter what, just keep showing up for yourself, even if it seems like it's hopeless.

Acknowledgments

To be honest, if it wasn't for my friend Will (rest in peace), there would be no *Travel Light*. You see, it was Will who had gone nomadic the year before and inspired my nomadic adventure that began in 2018. As you may have noticed, Will also played a key role in the following stories:

Chance Encounters (page 75)
The Good Parts (page 85)
Flirting (page 114)
The Stiffest Yogi (page 137)

My friend Koya was the one who coined the title *Travel Light*, after I mentioned that I wanted my next book to be about my experiences with nomading and minimalism. As soon as she heard the idea, she blurted out, "Call it *Travel Light*," and my heart voice confirmed, "That's the title!"

I then told my editor, Diana (from my previous book, *Knowing Where to Look*), about the idea for *Travel Light*. And ironically, she had been inspired to go nomadic after editing my last book—so naturally she was on board with the mission. And I continue to be so grateful to Diana for helping me turn my quirky book ideas into reality.

My wonderful agent, Coleen, helped to secure the publishing deal for *Travel Light* and began shepherding me through the series of deadlines. Without her gentle guidance and confidence in my ability to bring my words to the page, the idea for *Travel Light* would still be just that—an idea.

Meanwhile, due to the pandemic, I had relocated to an Airbnb in Mexico City in January 2021, where most of *Travel Light* was written. In between walking my 10,000 steps a day, working out with my resistance bands, and cafe hopping, I met as often as I could with Simona von Woikowsky over Zoom.

Simona is responsible for all of the beautiful illustrations you see in the book, including the cover illustration. We connected serendipitously after I announced on social media that I was in search of an illustrator who is as obsessed with the color blue as I am.

Following her heart voice, Simona reached out to me and shyly offered her services. As soon as I laid eyes on her work, my heart voice told me that she was the perfect illustrator for the job. And I couldn't be happier with the way the art turned out in *Travel Light*. True masterpieces.

I also want to acknowledge Tami, Rachael, and the rest of the team at Sounds True for giving me carte blanche to create the book of my dreams, from concept to title to cover to launch. You all are still the best publishing team I've worked with, and I'm continually inspired by how you put so much heart and spirit into the books you produce.

I also want to acknowledge my own personal Yoda, Maharishi Vyasananda Saraswati, who taught me Vedic meditation in 2003—an experience that transformed my relationship with the practice of meditation, helping me to become an enthusiastic daily meditator, and inspiring me to train as a meditation teacher in 2007 so I could share meditation with the world.

Sending a special thanks to Bryndan, Chris, Ava, and the fellas in the King's Council for your never-ending support while I was writing this book. And finally, I'd like to thank my immediate and extended family for all of your love and support. I feel so blessed to come from such a strong tribe of humans, and I'm honored to represent the Watkins family name in all that I do.

About the Author

LIGHT WATKINS has been a meditation and spiritual teacher for over twenty years. He is the author of *The Inner Gym*, *Bliss More*, and *Knowing Where to Look*. Light hosts a weekly podcast about purpose called *The Light Show* and an online community centered around "inner work" called The Happiness Insiders. Light travels the world giving talks and leading workshops on enlightened leadership, happiness, and meditation. He's been profiled in *Time*, *Vogue*, *Forbes*, *People*, and the *New York Times*. For more, visit lightwatkins.com.

About Sounds True

SOUNDS TRUE is a multimedia publisher whose mission is to inspire and support personal transformation and spiritual awakening. Founded in 1985 and located in Boulder, Colorado, we work with many of the leading spiritual teachers, thinkers, healers, and visionary artists of our time. We strive with every title to preserve the essential "living wisdom" of the author or artist. It is our goal to create products that not only provide information to a reader or listener but also embody the quality of a wisdom transmission.

For those seeking genuine transformation, Sounds True is your trusted partner. At SoundsTrue.com you will find a wealth of free resources to support your journey, including exclusive weekly audio interviews, free downloads, interactive learning tools, and other special savings on all our titles.

To learn more, please visit SoundsTrue.com/freegifts or call us toll-free at 800.333.9185.

sounds true
WAKING UP THE WORLD